OSPREY COMBAT AIRCR

Su-25 'FROGFOOT' UNITS IN COMBAT

SERIES EDITOR TONY HOLMES

OSPREY COMBAT AIRCRAFT 109

Su-25 'FROGFOOT' UNITS IN COMBAT

ALEXANDER MLADENOV

OSPREY PUBLISHING

Front Cover

A Russian Air Force Su-25 from 960th ShAP, home-based at Primorsko-Akhtarsk, attacks a target with S-24 240 mm rockets during the second campaign in Chechnya. At the height of the conflict, fought between September 1999 and August 2000, the colourful 'Frogfoots' of 960th ShAP were forward deployed to Mozdok. From here they fought alongside two Su-25 regiments of 1st GShAD, 461st ShAP and 368th ShAP.

The largest strike mission involving the 'Frogfoot' during the second Chechen campaign was conducted on 27 September 1999, just four days before the launch of the Russian ground offensive into Chechnya itself. This evolution involved Su-25s from all three regiments of 1st GShAD, which were secretively gathered at Mozdok. As many as 60 jets were scrambled in a single wave and in complete radio silence, tasked with mounting a devastating strike against a number of pre-planned targets. One of the pilots involved in this mission was Mikhail Pavlov of 461st ShAP, a combat-experienced Su-25 veteran who had participated in both Chechen campaigns (the first had been fought in 1994). He recalled:

'When approaching Chechnya to attack pre-planned targets, the Su-25 pairs and flights maintained a cruising altitude of between 12,500 ft and 16,730 ft. When initiating the attack, the pilot rolled the aircraft over into a 45- to 60-degree dive so as to ensure accuracy with his bombs or rockets. The Su-25's ASP-17BTs-8 electro-optical sight was used in the manual aiming mode only, without any automatic corrections, while the Klyon-PS laser designator/rangefinder was not employed due to the significant ranging errors associated with its use over mountainous terrain.' (*Cover artwork by Gareth Hector*)

Previous pages
In the all-new security environment following the break-up of the Soviet Union in December 1991, the small and robust Su-25 has gradually but indisputably emerged as the most useful aircraft of its generation in RuAF service, with between 350 and 400 on strength in the early 1990s. By the late 2000s, however, the active 'Frogfoot' fleet had been reduced to about 200 aircraft (*Andrey Zinchuk collection via Author*)

First published in Great Britain in 2015 by Osprey Publishing
PO Box 883, Oxford, OX1 9PL, UK
PO Box 3985, New York, NY 10185-3985, USA

E-mail: info@ospreypublishing.com

Osprey Publishing is part of the Osprey Group

© 2015 Osprey Publishing Limited

All rights reserved. Apart from any fair dealing for the purpose of private study, research, criticism or review, as permitted under the Copyright, Design and Patents Act 1988, no part of this publication may be reproduced, stored in a retrieval system, or transmitted in any form or by any means, electronic, electrical, chemical, mechanical, optical, photocopying, recording or otherwise without prior written permission. All enquiries should be addressed to the publisher.

A CIP catalogue record for this book is available from the British Library

ISBN: 978 1 4728 0567 6
PDF e-book ISBN: 978 1 4728 0568 3
e-Pub ISBN: 978 1 4728 0569 0

Edited by Tony Holmes and Phil Jarrett
Cover Artwork by Gareth Hector (www.garethhector.co.uk/aviation-art/)
Aircraft Profiles by Rolando Ugolini
Index by Alison Worthington
Originated by PDQ Digital Media Solutions, UK
Printed in China through World Print Ltd

15 16 17 18 19   10 9 8 7 6 5 4 3 2 1

Osprey Publishing is supporting the Woodland Trust, the UK's leading woodland conservation charity, by funding the dedication of trees.

www.ospreypublishing.com

CONTENTS

CHAPTER ONE
SOVIET 'JET *SHTURMOVIK*' 6

CHAPTER TWO
OPERATION *ROMB* 10

CHAPTER THREE
OPERATION *EXAMEN* 15

CHAPTER FOUR
378th OShAP OPERATIONS 22

CHAPTER FIVE
ACTION AFTER SOVIET BREAK UP 59

CHAPTER SIX
CHECHNYA AND SOUTH OSSETIA 70

CHAPTER SEVEN
EXPORT Su-25s IN COMBAT 81

CHAPTER EIGHT
CURRENT CONFLICTS 87

APPENDICES 92
COLOUR PLATES COMMENTARY 93
INDEX 96

CHAPTER ONE

SOVIET 'JET SHTURMOVIK'

The Sukhoi Su-25 was designed as an effective and survivable attack workhorse, expressly to fly short-range, low-level battlefield close-air-support (CAS) missions. In the 1980s and 1990s the type, also known by its NATO reporting name 'Frogfoot', proved a powerful and cost-effective weapon, being widely employed in counterinsurgency (COIN) operations worldwide and performing well in its dangerous role.

The Su-25 originated in a concept produced by a group of forward-thinking engineers at the Sukhoi Design Bureau, led by chief designers Oleg Samoilovich and Yuri Ivashetchkin. In March 1968 they produced some conceptual preliminary designs, originally inspired by Ivan Savtchenko, a teacher at the Yuri Gagarin Soviet Air Force Academy who specialised in research into frontal aviation combat employment tactics. Savtchenko was the first Soviet military expert to formulate a set of specific requirements for a new-generation affordable and lethal CAS aircraft to be built in large numbers, just like its World War 2 predecessors, the legendary piston-engined Ilyushin Il-2 *Shturmovik* and its improved derivative, the Il-10. Savtchenko's novel concept called for development of an all-new, eight-tonne, twin-engined light attack jet optimised for low-level operations. It was provisionally named the Light Army Attack Aircraft.

In late March 1969 the Soviet Ministry of Aviation Industry formally requested that Sukhoi prepare its proposal for a new-generation turbojet-powered attack aircraft. This was in fact an announcement of the formal tender for the development of a new aircraft for the Soviet Air Force (*Voenno-Vozdushnye Sily*, or VVS) in which Sukhoi initially competed

The T8-1 prototype made its maiden flight on 22 February 1975 and saw extensive use in the so-called 'factory testing' (manufacturer's trials) of the type completed in November of that same year, showing a promising performance. The new aircraft, however, required re-engining and a fuselage redesign in order to fully meet the VVS specification in terms of warload, range and speed. After an extensive rework lasting some 18 months, the enhanced first prototype, re-designated T8-1D, took the air for the first time in its new guise on 21 June 1978. Stage A of the aircraft's joint State testing effort was completed on 30 May 1980, and the more comprehensive Stage B finished on 30 December that same year. Both stages required as many as 186 sorties to be flown in total (*Sukhoi Company*)

The T8-4 prototype, appropriately numbered 'Red 84', was the second example built at the GAZ-31 factory in Tbilisi. It is seen here loaded with two B8M rocket packs, four FAB-250 250 kg HE bombs and two PTB-800 800-litre external fuel tanks. It took to the air for the first time in September 1979 and actively participated in the Su-25's extensive flight testing and evaluation. Retired in 1984, the T8-4 was handed over to the Moscow Aviation Institute to serve as a ground instructional airframe (*Sukhoi Company*)

against the Mikoyan, Yakovlev and Ilyushin design bureaux. The aircraft was required to be simple, affordable, easy to produce and maintain, and to have a high degree of combat survivability. The specification called for an all-new jet with a combat-manoeuvring speed of between 300 and 500 mph, a normal payload of 1000 kg (2200-lb), a maximum payload of 3000 kg (6600-lb) and a range at ground level of no less than 465 miles.

Sukhoi's attack aircraft concept was further improved to meet the requirements of the VVS technical specification in terms of speed and manoeuvrability. Given the internal Sukhoi Design Bureau designation T8, the project successfully passed the first phase of the competition and was shortlisted for the second, competing against the Mikoyan Design Bureau's MiG-21LSh proposal. All other candidates were rejected on technical grounds. In the event the Sukhoi project was quickly declared the winner in the second phase of the competition, as in 1971 the Mikoyan Design Bureau had decided to discontinue its participation for various internal reasons.

At the same time the VVS had insisted that the new attack aircraft have a higher speed than that originally proposed – no less than 750 mph when carrying four underwing B8M rocket pods. The maximum speed proposed by Sukhoi, however, was constrained to 560 mph so as to avoid having to use hydraulic boosters in the aircraft's control system in order to achieve reasonable control column forces in the pitch and roll axes. In the event the agreed maximum speed was 620 mph, which translated into Mach 0.82 at low level.

The first prototype, designated the T8-1, was completed by the end of 1974, and shortly thereafter it was declared ready to begin ground and flight testing. The aircraft made its maiden flight on 22 February 1975, with famous Sukhoi chief test pilot Vladimir Ilyushin at the controls.

In May 1977 the Sukhoi Design Bureau unveiled the representative production version of the T8. Compared with the prototypes, the definitive Su-25 (as the aircraft was designated by the VVS) attack jet had a lengthened fuselage, increased-span wings and a taller fin, as well as new Soyuz/Gavrilov R-95Sh non-afterburning turbojets in enlarged nacelles, an armoured 'bathtub' for the pilot and a new VPU-17A gun pack with a built-in GSh-30 (AO-17B) 30 mm twin-barrelled cannon.

In the summer of 1978 the first production-standard jet, designated T8-3, was completed and rolled out at the production plant at Tbilisi, in the then Soviet republic of Georgia. The type completed its expanded flight test programme in December 1980, and the following year it was launched into large-scale production. The aeroplane was not formally commissioned into VVS service until April 1987, however.

COMBAT SURVIVABILITY FEATURES

The T8's airframe was a very robust structure incorporating extensive system redundancy in an effort to achieve sufficient resistance to small-arms fire and high-speed missile warhead fragments. The combat survivability features, as incorporated in the design of the basic aircraft built before mid-1987, accounted for some 7.5 per cent of the aircraft's normal takeoff weight, or 600 kg (1320-lb), while Su-25s built after mid-1987 – the so-called 10th Series production standard – had vastly enhanced protection for the airframe and engines, accounting for 11.5 per cent of the aircraft's normal takeoff weight, some 1100 kg (2430-lb).

The principal combat survivability features included a deep armoured 'bath' for the pilot made from welded titanium alloy plates with a thickness of between 10 mm and 24 mm. These were capable of withstanding hits by up to 50 20 mm or 23 mm projectiles without developing cracks. The flat bulletproof windscreen, 70 mm thick, could withstand hits from 12.7 mm projectiles. The pilot's K-36L ejection seat had an armoured headrest that provided protection from bullets and high-speed missile warhead fragments coming from above and behind.

The airframe had damage-resistant load-bearing members and the control system used large-diameter pushrods (up to 40 mm) instead of cables as linkages for actuation of the control surfaces. The fitment of pushrods gave the Su-25 a high level of redundancy and hardening in case of mechanical damage by projectiles/high-speed fragments or fire. The pushrods could withstand direct hits by 12.7 mm rounds, and those connected to the elevators were made dual-redundant. The control runs were widely separated to avoid simultaneous damage by the same projectile or by fire ravaging inside the fuselage. In 1986 new-design steel pushrods with greatly increased resistance to fire were introduced, replacing the original titanium units that had proved vulnerable to fire damage.

An Su-25UB pilot fires the VPU-17A gun-pack, which contains a GSh-30 30 mm twin-barrel gun and 250 rounds – the weapon has a rate of fire of 3000 rounds per minute. Seasoned 'Frogfoot' pilots have remarked that the VPU-17A proved to be an irreplaceable weapon on certain occasions, thanks to its high accuracy. For instance, a well-trained pilot could shoot at will into randomly selected windows of a multi-storey building. When the Su-25 was being flown in a war zone, VVS and RuAF armours usually loaded the weapon's magazine with mixed ammunition, comprising fragmentation/HE, fragmentation/HE/tracer or armour-piercing/tracer rounds (*U-UAP via Author*)

The R-95Sh engines were also widely separated, being five feet apart, and 5 mm thick stainless-steel screens were installed between them and the fuselage to prevent simultaneous damage of both engines from a single missile warhead detonation, or a hit by a high-speed projectile. The screens also prevented fire from a damaged engine spreading to the good one.

Reticulated polyurethane foam, for explosive wave and fire suppression, occupied some 70 per cent of the volume of the fuel tanks. The tanks were lined with 20 mm thick double-layer porous resin protectors to prevent large fuel leaks when punctured by projectiles or high-speed fragments. The collector tank was also protected by 8 mm steel plating on the bottom and rear walls, while its side walls were made from 18 mm aluminium alloy plating.

In 10th Series aircraft only, extensive fire protection was provided by means of heat insulation screens housed in the tail, engine nacelles and internal bays adjacent to the fuel tanks, as well as a two-stage fire extinguishing system inside the engine bays.

All the basic items of equipment relating to the flight controls and fuel system were armour protected. The enhanced protection package, introduced in mid-1987 on 10th Series Su-25s, included 17 mm of titanium plating under the belly to protect the fuel lines feeding the engines, and a 17 mm-thick titanium plate on the starboard engine cowling to shield the oil tank and its pump control unit. The ASO-2V chaff/flare dispenser units next to the fin were also provided with 5 mm armour screens to protect against high-speed missile warhead fragments from behind. Finally, additional 18 mm armour plates were scabbed on to the hatches of the nose equipment bays.

This Su-25 sports a classical 1970s-vintage blue-grey cockpit filled with conventional 'steam gauge' analogue instruments, switches and selectors. Pilots described it as being roomy, comfortable and well laid out ergonomically (*Andrey Zinchuk collection via Author*)

PRODUCTION DATA

As many as 630 Su-25s (given the NATO reporting name 'Frogfoot-A') were built for the VVS between 1979 and 1991 at the Georgia-based factory known during Soviet times as Aviation Plant No 31 (GAZ-31), named after leading Bulgarian communist Georgy Dimitrov and now known as Tbilisi Aerospace Manufacturing (TAM). Within this number was a batch of 50 Su-25BMs with improved navigation equipment and powered by increased-thrust Tumanski R-195 engines. The factory also completed 185 Su-25Ks for export during this period. Around 160 of these were delivered to customers abroad through to 1989, with the remainder being taken on strength by the VVS. An additional 110 Su-25UB/UBK 'Frogfoot-B' two-seaters rolled off the line at the aviation plant in Ulan-Ude (U-UAP) in Russia.

In the 1980s a batch of 12 Su-25T specialised 'tankbusters' was built at TAM for test and evaluation purposes. In the 1990s and 2000s the factory, now in the independent state of Georgia, is known to have produced a few Su-25UM two-seaters, using incomplete Su-25T airframes. An additional 15 to 20 classic Su-25 'Frogfoot-As', powered by uprated R-195 turbojets, were also delivered.

CHAPTER TWO
OPERATION *ROMB*

Even before the T8 had completed Stage A of exhaustive joint State tests, conducted by the VVS Scientific Research Institute at Akhtubinsk to prove that the new attack aircraft met the required technical, flight and combat employment specifications, the Soviet Ministry of Defence had decided that it should be tested in combat. In fact this initiative was personally promoted by the Minister of Defence, Marshal of the Soviet Union Dmitriy Ustinov. Two prototypes, the T8-1D and the T8-3, were promptly modified by Sukhoi and deployed to Shindand airfield in Afghanistan to undergo the demanding combat employment testing phase codenamed Operation *Romb* (Rombus). Once in-theatre, the aircrafts' weapons sighting equipment would be evaluated, as would their ordnance and flight/navigation equipment, overall effectiveness of weapons delivery, and maintainability in real-world operational conditions.

Both the T8-1D and T8-3 were limited to a maximum speed of 560 mph and to up to 5g in manoeuvring. Modifications made to the prototypes before their deployment to Afghanistan included removal of some of the test instrumentation and installation of updated mission avionics, and filling the fuel tanks with reticulated foam to prevent explosion of the kerosene vapours in the event of a hit by incendiary rounds.

Fast-track field evaluation and testing of the T8 during Operation *Romb* was carried out under so-called 'peculiar conditions', as real-world war conditions are referred to in official Sukhoi Design Bureau and VVS documentation. The sorties completed in-theatre were considered to be an integral part of the so-called Stage B of the Su-25's flight test programme. Thus the promising 'Frogfoot' received its baptism of fire just five years after the aircraft's maiden flight.

DEPLOYMENT

The two modified prototypes were deployed to Shindand airfield on 18 April 1980, less than six months after the Soviet invasion of Afghanistan. During the ferry flight from Akhtubinsk, which commenced on 17 April, the aircraft maintained close formation with a Tupolev Tu-16 bomber that performed the role of group leader. Two refuelling stops were made, at Krasnovodsk and Mari, the jets staying overnight at the latter location. The next day the prototypes flew the last leg of the ferry flight to Shindand.

The crews involved in the operation included two test pilots drawn from Sukhoi, Alexander Ivanov and Nikolay Sadovnikov, and two more supplied by the VVS's Scientific Research Institute, Vladimir Solovyov and Valeriy Muzika.

After landing at Shindand, the new and still secret prototypes were immediately hidden within earthen revetments that had been covered by camouflage nets in an effort to conceal the presence of the test and evaluation team at the crowded airfield.

A significant number of Sukhoi test engineers were also deployed with the T8s, together with more technical personnel despatched by the design

The T8-1D was one of two 'Frogfoot' prototypes deployed to Afghanistan during Operation *Romb*, the latter taking place between 18 April and 6 June 1980 from Shindand airfield. *Romb* was an initiative promoted by the Minister of Defence, Marshal of the Soviet Union Dmitriy Ustinov. Two prototypes, the T8-1D and the T8-3, were promptly modified by Sukhoi for despatch to Afghanistan to undergo the demanding combat employment testing phase, evaluating the accuracy of the sighting equipment, a wide range of unguided ordnance, the flight/navigation equipment and the aircraft's overall maintainability and reliability in real-world operational conditions (*Sukhoi Company*)

bureaux responsible for the development of the aircraft's navigation and sighting equipment. The commanding officer of Operation *Romb*, Maj Gen Vladimir Alfyorov, then Deputy Chief of the VVS's Scientific Test Institute (Flight Test Centre), recalled;

'Despite the high levels of secrecy surrounding the deployment to Shindand, the personnel involved in the operation went about their work with great enthusiasm. They were all united by a common objective – to test and evaluate the brand-new jets in real-world combat conditions so as to reveal any design shortcomings of the equipment and weapons. This method of field testing was undertaken so to allow the VVS to avoid the huge losses that it could have suffered in a future large-scale conflict should the aircraft have had major shortcomings.

'The T8 was a state-of-the-art attack aircraft from a class that had been absent in our fleet since World War 2. It was intended to be, and eventually became, the baseline aircraft of the Soviet Union's frontal attack aviation force, boasting high performance – its top speed was 620 mph, the maximum war load reached four tonnes and the combat radius stretched to 218 miles. Furthermore, the T8 was capable of employing all air-to-ground ordnance approved for use by the VVS. It was able, for instance, to takeoff with eight underwing pylons loaded with eight 500 kg (1110-lb) or 32 100 kg (220-lb) bombs, as well as up to 256 57 mm rockets [housed in eight 32-round packs]. The T8 could also employ laser-guided air-to-surface missiles [ASMs] as well as air-to-air missiles [AAMs] on the outermost wing pylons.

'The T8 featured a purposely designed combat survivability package, comprising a welded titanium armoured bathtub for the pilot, explosion-proof fuel tanks, dual-redundant and protected flight control runs and engines separated from the fuselage by armour plating. In addition, the pilot wore a protective vest, armoured arm protectors and an armoured helmet.'

The first T8 familiarisation sorties in Afghan skies were flown on 21 April 1980. Initially, only test and evaluation flights were carried out in a bid to explore the accuracy of the aircraft's sighting system when employing a wide range of unguided ordnance that had already been cleared for the type.

During the first test and evaluation sorties from Shindand it was discovered that the T8's sighting system suffered from a systematic error when calculating aiming solutions for both bomb drops and rocket firings against targets at high elevation – exceeding 3280 ft above sea level. The root cause for this error was the failure to incorporate the data on the target's altitude above sea level when calculating the rocket-firing/bomb-dropping solution. After this problem had been discovered the T8's sighting system was promptly modified with new algorithms, which eliminated the systematic error and improved accuracy. All the test and evaluation sorties involving the T8's ordnance were performed at a small firing range located some 35 miles from the airfield at an elevation of 6660 ft above sea level. A stone ring 82 ft in diameter was set up to serve as a calibrated target.

However, the Operation *Romb* team was not restricted to performing only test and evaluation sorties. The T8 prototypes were used in anger for the first time on 29 April, a mere 11 days after their arrival at Shindand, when they provided CAS for Soviet troops fighting the *Mujahedeen* (Afghan armed opposition fighters). The targets ordered for destruction were at a maximum distance of 199 miles from Shindand, in the Chakhcharan area. The T8s, flown by Alexander Ivanov and Valeriy Muzika, were tasked with providing CAS for units of the 5th Motorised Infantry Division involved in COIN operations. Maj Gen Alfyorov recalled the first real-world combat employment of the T8;

'The pilots returned from the mission very excited, so I had to relieve their stress by using a bottle of brandy taken from my personal reserve. Only after they had had a drink did they sit down to write their post-mission report.'

More combat missions followed on 30 April, when the T8 pair was again despatched to bomb targets in the Chakhcharan area after Soviet troops encountered stiff resistance from well entrenched armed local opposition groups. The T8s amassed a total of four combat sorties in two missions, the aircraft dropping eight FAB-500TS and four BetAB-500U concrete-penetrating bombs to destroy hardened firing positions built into a steep slope. The targets were hit on the second mission, as all the bombs dropped during the first had missed.

On 7 May, during the second combat sortie of the day, both pilots reported communications problems with ground forces in the assigned target area. Having failed to establish contact with the troops on the ground, they eventually decided to return to base, dropping their bombs in an uninhabited mountainous area. The next day the T8s repeated the mission, logging a total of four sorties against *Mujahedeen* fighters hiding in a cave complex in the Luarkoh Valley, some 18 miles from the city of Farakh. The first mission saw the 'Frogfoots' expend eight OFAB-100-120 100 kg high-explosive/fragmentation bombs and eight UB-32M rocket packs containing a total of 256 S-5 57 mm projectiles in 12 shallow-dive attack passes. The T8s began their attacks at 5250 ft and pulled out at 660 ft. After the mission the pilots reported four direct rocket hits into the cave entrances, while five of the bombs had impacted the ground just above the caves and sealed them up with falling rocks and debris.

During the second combat mission that day the pair dropped eight OFAB-100-120 and eight FAB-500 bombs in six passes. Their primary aim was to detonate *Mujahedeen* mines planted in a narrow gorge, although enemy fighters occupying hardened defensive positions in a nearby cave complex were also targeted. A direct bomb hit was reported to have caused a large secondary explosion inside one of the caves that was being used as a storage depot for explosives and ammunition. It later transpired that this particular complex was a well-equipped *Mujahedeen* logistics camp used to support anti-government operations across the province.

On 9 May the T8 prototypes flew two more combat sorties each in the Farakh region. There were no forward air controllers (FACs) in the area, and the infantry units on the ground attempted some makeshift methods for directing the aircraft by firing small arms and artillery in the direction of the enemy in the hope that the pilots would spot the tracers aimed at the enemy positions that were to be attacked. The lack of proper FAC support during the CAS missions flown in the previous days had significantly reduced the T8s' combat effectiveness, and this had prompted Maj Gen Alfyorov to spend a lot of time setting up better coordination and cooperation with the troops in the field.

On 11 May the T8s conducted two more combat missions against targets situated 22 miles east of Farakh. As usual, the targets were in a mountainous area, but this time the location of the enemy positions was pinpointed by the reconnaissance battalion of the 5th Motorised Infantry Division. Each T8

Operation *Romb*'s CO, Maj Gen Vladimir Alfyorov, then Deputy Chief of the VVS's Scientific Test Institute (Flight Test Centre) congratulates VVS test pilot Valeriy Muzika (right) upon returning from his first T8 combat sortie in Afghanistan on 29 April 1980 (*I'ldar Bedredtinov archive via Author*)

was armed with four FAB-500 high-explosive (HE) bombs and four 20-round B8M pods loaded with 80 mm rockets. The second mission of the day, again to attack targets in the same area, saw the use of four BetAB-500 concrete-penetrating bombs and eight FAB-500TS bombs with hardened forward bodies to destroy well-protected enemy positions. Both types of bomb were used to good effect to destroy a hardened heavy machine gun nest and close the entrances of selected caves in the area that were occupied by enemy snipers. That same day the T8s were also called upon to perform two more test and evaluation sorties in the vicinity of Shindand.

On 12 May a lone T8, piloted by VVS test pilot V Muzika, performed an evaluation sortie at the aircraft's maximum combat radius, supported by an Antonov An-12 transport aircraft that was used as a radio relay platform and two Mil Mi-8 helicopters for combat search and rescue (C-SAR) assistance.

OPERATION *ROMB* RESULTS

During the 50-day evaluation period of Operation *Romb* the two T8 prototypes reportedly amassed 56 test and evaluation and 44 real-world combat sorties, logging 98 hours 11 minutes total flying time. Of these sorties, 30 were analysed as part of the type's state testing and evaluation effort. All of the test and evaluation sorties were completed by 16 May, which allowed the aircraft to continue flying real-world combat missions against the armed opposition forces until 5 June 1980.

Each holding a bouquet of flowers, Soviet Air Force test pilots Vladimir Solovyov (left) and Valeriy Muzika (right) are officially greeted at the Scientific Test Institute in Akhtubinsk upon their return from Operation *Romb*. The 50-day test and evaluation clearly demonstrated that the new attack aircraft was much better suited to the CAS role than all other Soviet jets deployed to Afghanistan, such as the Su-17 and MiG-21 (*I'ldar Bedredtinov archive via Author*)

The weapons used during the evaluation and combat sorties included 57 mm, 80 mm, 240 mm and 250 mm rockets and 100 kg (220-lb), 250 kg (550-lb) and 500 kg (1110-lb) free-fall bombs, as well as RBK-250-275 cluster bombs. BetAB-500 concrete-penetration bombs were also employed on several occasions to good effect. Among the most notable achievements reported during Operation *Romb* were the combat sorties flown with a maximum combat load of eight 500 kg FAB-500M62 HE bombs, as well as 32 100 kg OFAB-100-120 fragmentation/HE bombs.

The T8 demonstrated excellent hot-and-high performance and good aiming accuracy, as Sukhoi test pilot Alexander Ivanov, who participated in Operation *Romb*, recalled;

'The 500 kg bombs, when dropped by the Su-25, usually impacted within 33 ft of the bombsight's aiming mark on the target. The aircraft proved more than capable of performing aerobatics with 1000 kg of combat ordnance, demonstrating benign handling characteristics in this heavyweight configuration. The remarkable weapons delivery effectiveness of the Su-25 was also acknowledged by the ground forces.'

Some shortcomings were noted by the test pilots during Operation *Romb*, however, such as the time the R-95Sh engines took to go from idle to maximum power rating after the throttle levers were pushed fully forward. The ineffectiveness of the petal-type airbrakes fitted on the engine nacelles was also highlighted.

Overall, Operation *Romb* was judged to have been a success, with the aircraft's positive showing in combat proving that the T8 could perform the CAS role effectively in a hot-and-high operational environment over rugged terrain. The jet had also demonstrated satisfactory accuracy in bomb and rocket delivery, combined with unsurpassed manoeuvrability and takeoff and landing characteristics.

OPERATION *EXAMEN*

The first combat unit of the rejuvenated attack aviation fleet of the VVS's frontal aviation branch was 80th OShAP (*Otdel'niy Shturmovoy Aviatsionniy Polk* – Independent Attack Aviation Regiment), assigned to the Trans-Caucasian Military District. Formed in February 1981, this two-squadron regiment was stationed at Sital-Chai airfield in today's Azerbaijan, not far from the capital, Baku. The regiment immediately began work-ups for its scheduled combat deployment to Afghanistan, as the initial cadre of pilots had already been sent to the Lipetsk-based 4th Combat Training and Aircrew Conversion Centre in February 1981 for the theoretical part of the Su-25 conversion-to-type. Its first 'Frogfoots' were taken on strength on 14 April.

80th OShAP was tasked with training air- and groundcrews following an accelerated schedule that allowed the regiment to deploy a squadron-size combat unit to Afghanistan as soon as possible. Once in-theatre the unit would undertake a formal large-scale evaluation of the Su-25 in real-world combat conditions. This event was codenamed Operation *Examen* (Exam).

By May 1981 80th OShAP had a fleet of 11 production-standard Su-25s and one experimental aircraft, the T8-6, equipping one squadron, these jets receiving consecutive serials from 01 through to 12. After the unit had completed the flight training component of the conversion-to-type course at Sital-Chai, the VVS command authorities had ordered the formation of a new squadron-size independent combat unit for permanent deployment to the Afghan war theatre. Designated 200th OShAE (*Otdel'naya Shturmovay Aviatsionnaya Eskadrilya* – Independent Attack Aviation Squadron), it was staffed by trained personnel drawn from 80th OShAP and commanded by Lt Col Alexander Afanasyev. The unit also inherited the 12 Su-25s originally taken on strength by the regiment.

The newly formed independent squadron and its entire fleet of Su-25s (plus two Su-17UM3 swing-wing two-seaters intended for familiarisation and check flights) arrived at Shindand airfield on 12 June 1981. The unit was declared combat-ready on 9 July, and on that date it flew its first operational sorties in the Luarkoh area in support of a COIN operation by the Soviet Army's 5th Motorised Rifle Division. The newly arrived Su-25s provided on-demand CAS, and also delivered air strikes against pre-planned targets.

AFGHANISTAN WAR THEATRE

Su-25s were in Afghanistan as a direct result of Soviet intervention in the country's civil war in late 1979. Throughout that year the Marxist government in Kabul had repeatedly asked for increased military support and direct Soviet involvement. In the autumn of 1979 Afghanistan's Prime Minister, Hafizullah Amin, formally asked the Soviet Union to intervene with military force in an effort to suppress the armed opposition and strengthen his regime. The Soviet government relented and made the fateful decision to despatch a limited military contingent to invade Afghanistan. The nation's hard-line Marxist regime had already faced a particularly fierce armed opposition that had achieved effective control over most of the country.

Soviet military units entered Kabul on 24 December 1979, and instead of helping Amin they quickly replaced his regime with a new puppet government. At the time the Soviet Union saw the internal crisis in Afghanistan as an opportunity to expand its area of influence in Central Asia. In the event the Soviet Army's almost ten-year-long occupation of Afghanistan proved clearly ineffective in stabilising the country and suppressing the armed opposition, which was generously supported by the Western world and a handful of resourceful Islamic countries. In fact the Soviet intervention only aggravated Afghanistan's bloody internal conflict. As a result, by the early 1980s, the Soviet military machine found itself engaged in a protracted and rather bloody war of attrition that it was subsequently unable to win.

Most of the missions flown by 200th OShAE were performed either in the southern regions of Afghanistan around Kandahar or in northern areas of the country, specifically in the notorious Pandjsher Valley, where the Soviet Army launched as many as 12 offensives but proved unable to establish effective control. Although the Su-25s were typically loaded with two 800-litre external tanks to extend their combat radius up to 248 miles, this was still barely enough fuel to enable them to reach targets in the Kandahar area while operating from Shindand. In order to be able to attack targets in the Pandjsher Valley, however, the Su-25s had to be deployed to forward airfields such as Bagram and Kabul that were closer to the target area.

Initially, 200th OShAE's Su-25s were used in composite formations, flying combat missions with the Su-17s of 217th APIB (*Aviatsionniy Polk Istrebiteley-Bombardirovshtikov* Aviation Regiment of Fighter-Bombers), also based at Shindand. When operating in mixed packages attacking pre-planned targets the Su-17s were used to detect and mark the targets with smoke bombs. They also suppressed the *Mujahedeen's* anti-aircraft weaponry, represented at that time largely by DShK 12.7 mm heavy machine guns captured from government forces. A minute after the Su-17s had made their strafing pass, two or three pairs of Su-25s would arrive over the target to drop bombs on the smoke markers.

When attacking targets in mountainous areas Su-25 pilots used the tactic of surprise, operating in one or two pairs. The leader attacked first, while the wingman covered him from above – in the second attack pass they switched roles. The Su-25's agility allowed pilots to mount each subsequent attack from a different direction, even against targets in narrow valleys.

Another typical mission for the Su-25 was the free-hunting (search-and-destroy or armed reconnaissance-strike) patrol, aimed at knocking out moving targets of opportunity in predetermined areas – usually *Mujahedeen* re-supply convoys. Su-25 pairs or four-aircraft flights involved in such missions usually flew at altitudes of between 1970 ft and 3940 ft while undertaking visual searches for enemy vehicles.

The S-24 240 mm rocket was a favourite weapon from the very beginning of the Su-25's combat use in Afghanistan. In its basic form, equipped with a contact fuse and warhead, the weapon had a good penetration capability that allowed it to destroy hardened targets. Upon detonation the rocket broke up into more than 4000 fragments that had a lethal radius of up to 130 ft. The weapon could also be fitted with a proximity radar fuse that detonated the rocket 108 ft above the ground to ensure coverage of a much greater area when used against soft targets. This gave the S-24 a lethal radius of between 980 ft and 1300 ft (*Andrey Zinchuk* collection via Author)

Su-25 WEAPONRY

Initially, the S-5 family of 57 mm rockets were commonly used by Su-25s in Afghanistan, the weapons being fired from the UB-32M 32-round packs to knock out area targets. However, it was soon discovered that these simple and lightweight projectiles had low destructive power, especially in mountainous regions. The 57 mm rockets were duly replaced by the much more powerful, and accurate, S-8 80 mm rockets, fired from 20-round B8M packs.

S-24 240 mm rockets were mainly used to destroy point targets owing to their remarkably high accuracy and powerful high-explosive/fragmentation warhead, which weighed 120 kg (271-lb). Its optimum launch range was about 6560 ft, and the rocket could hit targets less than 50 ft in diameter. This made the weapon well suited to destroying hardened targets. The S-24 was later supplemented by the heavier and even more precise S-25 tube-launched rocket, which had a launch range of up to 13,120 ft. This weapon was produced in three separate versions with different warheads. The S-25O had a fragmentation warhead weighing 150 kg (330-lb), the projectile being fitted with a proximity radar fuse that detonated it between 16 ft and 66 ft above the ground, spreading 10,000 lethal fragments. The S-25OF had a more powerful fragmentation/blast warhead weighing 200 kg (427-lb), which was detonated by contact fuse. Finally, the S-25OFM boasted the largest fragmentation/blast warhead to give the weapon penetrating capability. Fitted with a contact fuse, it was capable of knocking out hardened targets.

The main types of general-purpose bombs used by the Su-25 in Afghanistan were the fragmentation/HE OFAB-100-120 and OFAB-250M54, as well as the more powerful blast-type FAB-500M56 or FAB-500M62 and RBK-250 and RBK-500 cluster bombs. Another commonly employed weapon was the ZB-500 napalm canister, used for attacking area targets.

The VPU-17A built-in gun pack was regarded as a last-ditch weapon, being rarely used in combat, while the podded twin-barrel GSh-23L cannon with 250 rounds in SPPU-22-01 gun pods was more frequently employed during the initial years of the war in Afghanistan.

In addition to the on-demand CAS, pre-planned strikes and free-hunting missions, the Su-25 was also widely deployed for aerial mine-laying. Secondary missions conducted on an occasional basis included escorting helicopter groups during large-scale assault operations, escorting vehicle convoys and visual aerial reconnaissance at low altitude, mainly pre- and post-strike.

The ordnance typically carried on long-range sorties with a radius of up to 186 miles from base included two to four 230 kg (550-lb) or 500 kg bombs or rocket pods and two external tanks. Without the latter, the Su-25 was restricted to operations against targets at a maximum radius of just 127 miles, and such missions were rare.

Some stringent operational restrictions were imposed on 200th OShAE Su-25s in the first years of the war, mainly owing to the aircraft's unreliable navigation equipment. As a consequence the 'Frogfoot' community was not permitted to fly combat sorties in bad weather or at night.

One of the Su-25's key strengths was the speed at which it could be serviced, pre-flight checked and re-armed. Indeed, a four-aircraft flight could be readied in just 25 minutes, while an eight-aircraft mission required just 40 minutes of preparation time. Nine or ten aircraft out of the 12 deployed by 200th OShAE were usually available for operations on a daily basis.

The Su-25 proved survivable enough for the ground attack role, and the results of operations by 200th OShAE during the first personnel rotation (which ran from 12 June 1981 to early October 1982) proved very positive. 'Frogfoot' pilots had routinely exploited the jet's unmatched agility by manoeuvring into narrow mountain valleys in order to deliver ordnance with precision – something that VVS Su-17M/M2 and MiG-21SM/bis fighter-bombers deployed to Afghanistan could rarely do. Pilots usually flew four or five sorties a day, but on some very intense days they flew up to eight combat sorties. During the first eight months of operations in-theatre 200th OShAP had completed 2000 combat missions and logged a total of 2136 hours, with each Su-25 averaging 178 hours per jet. No losses were reported, but on 12 occasions Su-25s had returned to base with one engine inoperative owing to damage from small-arms fire.

1st Series Su-25 '03' is seen taxiing out in front of the busy apron at Bagram in 1982. Visible in the background are MiG-21bis fighters of 927th IAP (*Istrebitel'nyy Aviatsionnaya Polk*** – Fighter Aviation Regiment) and Su-17M3Rs of 263rd ORAE (***Otdel'naya Razvedyvatel'naya Aviatsionnyy Eskadrilya*** – Independent Reconnaissance Aviation Squadron). The 'Frogfoot' is departing on a short-range mission, and therefore lacks external tanks. It is, however, laden with bombs and 80 mm rocket pods. Operating without external tanks was a very rare occurrence in Afghanistan owing to the aircraft's notoriously short mission radius and endurance on internal fuel alone (***Andrey Kozhemyakin archive via Author***)**

SECOND ROTATION PERIOD

The second rotation of 200th OShAE took place from September 1982 to early October 1983, and it involved air- and groundcrews that were again drawn from 80th OShAP, commanded by Maj Vladimir Khanarin. The new personnel deployed to Shindand in late September, the first familiarisation sorties were reported on 1 October and the first combat missions followed ten days later. Usually, one four-aircraft flight was assigned for strike missions, but two flights were sometimes required.

The unit remained equipped with 12 Su-25s, two brand new 'Frogfoots' having been sent out to replace the T8-6 experimental aircraft that returned to the Soviet Union in December 1981 to continue participating in the type's testing and evaluation and an Su-25 lost in a non-combat-related accident on the 14th of that same month.

In late 1982 the 500 kg ODAB-500P thermobaric or fuel/air explosive (FAE) bomb was introduced for use against enemy fighters in the open or concealed in shelters, trenches or mountain caves. The intense blast and heat created by the detonation of the liquid explosive after it had spread over the ground in a gaseous state and mixed with the air was so powerful that it could destroy an armoured personnel carrier (APC) in close proximity. After detonation, the initial blast wave directed outwards was followed by a secondary one moving in the opposite direction to cause an alternating destructive effect on targets. Another significant lethal effect of this type of bomb was that it consumed all the oxygen in the air within a certain radius, instantly killing everyone in the affected area. In addition, because of its powerful blast (said to be one-and-a-half to three times more powerful than that of HE bombs of the same weight), the ODAB-500P was widely employed to clear minefields when preparing landing zones for helicopter-borne assault parties.

Pilots involved in the second rotation flew most of their combat missions from forward operating bases closer to the principal target areas – mostly from Bagram (for five months) and Kandahar (for two months). In addition, 200th OShAP aircrews conducted numerous so-called 'shuttle' missions, taking off from their permanent base at Shindand to lay mines on a number of mountain trails around Kabul, before landing at Bagram to refuel and rearm.

The first article in the West's specialised aviation press about the new Soviet attack aircraft operating in Afghanistan appeared in the 2 December 1982 issue of *Flight International* magazine. Headlined 'Frogfoot in action against Afghan rebels', it revealed that British journalists from an Independent Television (ITV) team visiting the territories held by the *Mujahedeen* had managed to photograph Su-25s while they were bombing a village in Afghanistan. The new attack jet was described as the Soviet equivalent of the Fairchild A-10, but bearing a close resemblance to Northrop's A-9, which had lost out to the A-10 in the USAF's AX competition. The British journalist who took the photographs told *Flight International* that the Su-25 attacks appeared to have taken place from fairly high altitude, the 'Frogfoot' pilots apparently being reluctant to enter the steep-sided Afghan valleys. Nigel Ryan, producer of the ITV programme 'Afghanistan: behind Russian lines', who had observed the Su-25 attacks at close range, noted that the bombing was not very accurate.

FIRST LOSS

The biggest problem Su-25 pilots encountered in the air during the aircraft's early years of regular operation in Afghanistan was caused by a well-known inherent design shortcoming, namely poor controllability in bank (while rolling) at high speeds owing to excessive control column forces induced by the manually actuated ailerons. As previously noted, this had caused severe operating limitations – a maximum speed of 530 mph and turning limited to 5g when manoeuvring – to be imposed during the T8's test and evaluation phase.

Ineffective ailerons were indeed to blame for 200th OShAE's first Su-25 loss, on 14 December 1981. Capt Mikhail Dyakov was unable to counter (by aileron deflection) the violent unintentional banking caused by non-symmetrical 500 kg (1100-lb) bomb separation in a diving attack while exceeding the 530 mph speed limitation. As a consequence, the uncontrollable aircraft (bearing the serial number '10') rolled upside down, failed to pull out from the dive and hit the ground, killing Dyakov – he had not attempted to bail out. The crash had initially been attributed to enemy heavy machine gun fire, but after analysing the data retrieved from the aircraft's Tester-U3 magnetic-type crash-survivable flight data recorder it was discovered that the loss of control in bank was the principal cause.

The second Su-25 loss happened during the second personnel rotation, in April 1983, and this too was not as a result of enemy action. A fully combat-laden 'Frogfoot' flown by the squadron's Deputy CO (Political Affairs), Maj A Shatilov, stalled immediately after takeoff owing to control system failure. The Su-25, carrying four FAB-500 bombs, rapidly lost height and crashed. The pilot ejected successfully from a height of 490 ft, however.

The second personnel rotation came to an end in early October 1983 following the arrival in-theatre of the third rotation during the latter half of September. Air- and groundcrew again came from 80th OShAP, and they were commanded by Maj Pyotr Ruban. Combat sorties were initiated in early October, with missions being flown with the original 1st Series Su-25s. That same month a brand-new 4th Series 'Frogfoot' was delivered to the squadron to replace the Su-25 lost in April, and another aircraft was returned to the plant at Tbilisi so that its fuselage could be repaired after it had suffered significant deformation following excessive fuel leakage.

In early January 1984 200th OShAE moved permanently to Bagram. Shortly thereafter, on the 16th, the unit suffered its third Su-25 loss in Afghanistan. During a four-aircraft mission to bomb hardened enemy positions near the city of Urgun, the jet flown by Maj Ruban was hit by a surface-to-air missile (SAM) – a Soviet-made 9K32 Strela-2M (NATO reporting name SA-7 'Grail') – while pulling up after a bombing run. The missile caused serious damage to the control system and engines, and the aircraft entered an uncontrollable roll. Ruban tried to eject as the bank angle reached almost 90 degrees, but it was too late and at a too low an altitude. The parachute failed to deploy as a result, and Ruban received fatal injuries when he hit the ground.

For his outstanding combat achievements Maj Pyotr Ruban was posthumously promoted to lieutenant colonel and awarded the Soviet Union's highest military honour, the Golden Star of Hero of the Soviet Union. His award report noted that, during his brief combat career, which included 106 combat sorties totalling 96 flying hours, Lt Col Ruban had

Maj Pyotr Ruban was CO of 200th OShAE's third personnel rotation with the Su-25 squadron in Afghanistan, which deployed to the war zone in October 1983. He was killed in action near Urgun on 16 January 1984 during an unsuccessful low-altitude ejection from his 1st Series Su-25 '13' after it had been badly damaged by a SAM hit. Ruban was posthumously awarded the Golden Star of Hero of the Soviet Union, thus becoming the first 'Frogfoot' pilot to receive the highest Soviet state award. Three more Su-25 pilots were presented with this decoration at later stages of the Afghanistan campaign for their outstanding combat exploits, one of them posthumously (*Author's collection – Aviatsia i Kosmonavtika*)

A typical scene on the ground during a 40th Army offensive operation in Afghanistan, involving assault transport helicopters provided with top cover and CAS support by Mi-24s and Su-25s (*Author's collection*)

Introduced for the first time in late 1984, the Grach (Rook) badge soon became the war-insignia of the 'Frogfoot' community in Afghanistan. It was applied to 378th OShAP's aircraft in a wide range of variations, mainly on the engine intakes (*Andrey Zinchuk collection via Author*)

led 13 missions against *Mujahedeen* positions, destroying as many as 14 DShK-12.7 heavy machine gun emplacements, three hardened defensive sites, six motor vehicles, two motorcycles, one fuel storage facility, more than 300 mines and three guns. It was also estimated that he had killed 250+ enemy combatants.

Following the loss of Maj Ruban, Maj Georgiy Chekhov was appointed the new squadron CO. Under his command 200th OShAE continued to conduct intensive combat operations, taking part in several large-scale offensives launched by Soviet forces. The first of these took place in the Pandjsher Valley in April 1984, and it was followed by three more operations around the capital, Kabul.

The fourth personnel rotation of 200th OShAE took place in late September 1984. This time air- and groundcrews came from the second VVS regiment to convert to the Su-25, 90th OShAP, which had received its first Su-25s in 1983. At the time it was stationed at Tiraspol airfield in the Odessa Military District (now in Moldova), although the regiment subsequently moved to Artsiz, in Ukraine.

This personnel rotation arrived at Bagram under the command of Lt Col Nikolay Shapovalov, bringing with it ten brand new 6th Series Su-25s that had only been delivered to the regiment in July and August. The pilots of the new rotation with 200th OShAE flew their initial combat missions under the supervision of experienced veterans from the third rotation, who eventually returned home to the Soviet Union on 30 September. The new aircrews of 200th OShAE had formally started independent combat operations three days earlier.

The squadron saw plenty of action with nine of its new 6th Series 'Frogfoots' (one had been badly damaged during the ferry flight), flying them alongside the seven surviving 1st Series aircraft for a number of months. 200th OShAE's fleet was further strengthened on 12 October by the arrival of four additional 6th Series Su-25s, and two more 5th Series examples followed not long after. All of the 5th and 6th Series Su-25s had hydraulically boosted ailerons, which increased the maximum speed limit to 620 mph and the maximum manoeuvring limit to 6.5g. These enhanced-capability 'Frogfoots' also had better airbrakes, preventing acceleration in dive attacks, dual-redundant nosewheel steering, an improved fuel system and engines with a longer time between overhauls. The new fleet reinforcements eventually allowed the worn-out 1st Series survivors to be withdrawn from use and sent back to the Soviet Union for overhaul. They departed Bagram on 18 October.

The fourth personnel rotation saw only brief service in Afghanistan with 200th OShAE, as in early November 1984 the squadron was disbanded and its entire fleet and all of its personnel were assigned to the newly established two-squadron attack regiment 378th OShAP, which was also stationed at Bagram.

378th OShAP OPERATIONS

378th OShAP was a brand-new attack regiment established on 5 November 1984, with a structure comprising a command section (headquarters), two component aviation squadrons and a field maintenance unit. 1st AE (*Aviatsionnaya Eskadrilya* – Aviation Squadron) was stationed at Bagram, inheriting the personnel of the disbanded 200th OShAE, together with the regiment's command section, while 2nd AE was permanently stationed at Kandahar. A batch of 12 additional 6th Series Su-25s, taken from 80th OShAP at Sital-Chai, and two Aero L-39Cs were ferried to Kandahar on the very day 378th OShAP was established, but four of these jets were soon redeployed to Bagram. The regiment's fleet initially consisted of 22 Su-25s (14 at Bagram and eight at Kandahar) and four L-39C two-seaters, which were used for familiarisation and check rides (two at Bagram and two at Kandahar).

The pilots and technicians of the newly established attack regiment, dedicated to operating in Afghanistan, were drawn from the two existing VVS frontline attack regiments at the time, 80th and 90th OShAPs. The regiment's CO during the first personnel rotation, which was in-theatre from 5 November 1984 to 12 October 1985, was Col Anatoliy Bakushev. During this rotation period 378th OShAP completed 10,500 combat sorties. The regimental operations report claims the destruction of 280 enemy strongholds/compounds and 20 defensive sites, inflicting huge manpower losses on the *Mujahedeen*.

A busy day at Bagram in the summer of 1985. Weapons ready for loading are seen in the foreground – 250 kg and 500 kg bombs on trolleys that were towed out to the 'Frogfoot' flightline (*Andrey Kojemyakin archive via Author*)

Most of the CAS sorties undertaken by the first rotation were flown at altitudes of between 1960 ft and 3280 ft above mountainous terrain, and the aircraft's extensive armour protection demonstrated good resistance to small-arms ground fire. Attacks from such low altitude offered excellent conditions for target recognition and sighting before expending rockets or releasing bombs. Consequently, the Su-25's multiple attack runs resulted in accurate hits, making the 'Frogfoot' a deadly effective CAS asset. During the first rotation, 378th OShAP's Su-25s took as many as 20 hits from 12.7 mm and 14.5 mm heavy machine guns, as well as from 7.62 mm assault rifles and machine guns. All of the damaged aircraft managed to return to base, where they were promptly repaired.

In October 1985 the regiment received a batch of four new 5th Series Su-25s, and shortly thereafter two more 7th Series examples arrived.

Su-25 '26' of 1st AE undergoes pre-flight servicing at Bagram. In front of the aircraft an FAB-500M54 500 kg bomb awaits loading onto the aircraft, which is also armed with a UB-32M 57 mm rocket pod (*Andrey Kozhemyakin archive via Author*)

CAS SPECIFICS

The on-demand CAS practised by the 'Frogfoot' community in Afghanistan was conducted in response to requests issued by troops in contact with the enemy. Dedicated FAC teams were assigned to each Soviet ground unit conducting operations in-theatre, at regimental, battalion and sometimes even company level, to manage the on-demand CAS tasks and direct the aircrafts' attacks. These FAC teams were always headed by aviation officers from the Combat Control Group, within the structure of the 40th Army's Aviation Command and Control (C^2) Centre.

When in fire contact with the enemy the ground commanders forwarded their requests for air support to the FAC team assigned to their unit, which, in turn, immediately called the Antonov An-26RT aerial command post that was airborne round the clock in the area of operations. In turn, the An-26RT mission commander immediately forwarded the received CAS request to the C^2 Centre at Bagram. If all the pre-conditions for issuing a go-clearance were met, the air assets on ground alert (Mil Mi-24 attack helicopters and/or Su-25s) received a mission order, also containing a brief instruction about the position of the troops requesting CAS and the general situation on the ground in the target area. On-demand CAS missions were usually conducted by a pair of Mi-24s or Su-25s sitting on the ground on quick reaction alert (QRA), required to be airborne within 15 minutes of receiving the order to go.

378th OShAP also conducted a significant number of pre-planned strike missions against enemy strongholds, re-supply bases and weapon/ammunition depots. On the most intensive days, between ten and twenty such strikes were launched. The regiment typically received the orders for these missions from the 40th Army's Aviation C^2 Centre the day before. The regimental CO, his staff and the squadron COs then undertook all the necessary mission planning, as well as scheduling the aircrews and the

CHAPTER FOUR

Seen at Mazar-e-Sharif airfield, Su-25 '34' is inspected after returning with combat damage from a mission on 4 August 1985. 1Lt T Kononenko had had to perform an emergency landing in the jet following an on-board fire caused by a single 7.62 mm bullet hitting the port engine intake and puncturing a fuel tank. The fire in the turbine area was started when leaking fuel entered the engine. Although the pilot was ordered to eject, he decided to activate the fire suppression system and land at the nearest airfield. A repair team sent to Mazar-e-Sharif managed to change the engine and repair the combat damage in just two days. A further three days were then spent completing a field repair that restored the jet's mission capabilities after it had been ferried to Bagram (*Andrey Kozhemyakin archive via Author*)

available aircraft, in an effort to allocate proper resources to all ordered strikes to be flown the next day. Most of the pre-planned missions were conducted in the early morning hours, just after dawn.

Free-hunting missions were also frequently undertaken by Su-25s, being conducted in areas with known enemy activity – most often along known roads and trails used by *Mujahedeen* re-supply convoys consisting of motor vehicles (pick-up trucks) or pack animals (camels, donkeys and horses). When suspicious activity on the ground was spotted, the leader of the pair reported to the Aviation C^2 Centre via the radio relay aircraft, which, in turn, had to confirm that there were no friendlies in the area and then authorise the attack.

For aerial mine-laying missions in Afghanistan the Su-25 carried two to four KMGU-2 mine-dispenser pods, each containing as many as 1248 PFM-1 anti-personnel mines. Once overhead the target area the 'Frogfoot' pilot flew straight-and-level legs at a height of 1300 ft and speed of 435 mph to 470 mph in order to disperse the mines as widely as possible. According to pilots who flew these missions in the Su-25, dispersing mines transversely in valleys was quite a difficult task. Furthermore, while flying straight and level at low altitude the jet was an easy target for *Mujahedeen* heavy machine guns and anti-aircraft artillery (AAA) pieces.

According to the volume *Su-25 Attack Aircraft – 30 Years In Service, Part I* by Andrey Kojemyakin and Andrey Korotkov, the percentages of the types of mission flown during the first personnel rotation of 378th OShAP were as follows – pre-planned strikes, 55 per cent; CAS, 30 per cent; aerial mine-laying, 12 per cent; free-hunting (reconnaissance-attack patrols), two per cent; other missions, one per cent (these missions included, for instance, escorting helicopters during large-scale assault landing operations and the protection of vehicle convoys).

378th OShAP reported two pilots and their aircraft lost in action during the first personnel rotation. In addition, it suffered two non-combat-related aircraft losses. The average number of sorties flown per aircraft during the 12-month-long combat period was 216, with the maximum being 315

378th OShAP's first pilot loss (and the third since the beginning of 'Frogfoot' operations in Afghanistan) occurred in unclear circumstances on 10 December 1984 during a CAS mission in the Pandjsher Valley. A likely cause was heavy machine gun fire, with hits possibly being taken within the cockpit while the pilot was performing his final strafing pass with the built-in 30 mm cannon after expending all of his bombs and rockets. Alternatively, the loss could have been caused by pilot error. Whatever the reason, the aircraft impacted the ground next Kidjol village in rebel-held territory. The body of 1Lt Vladimir Zazdravnov of 1st AE was not recovered from the crash site despite a C-SAR effort that continued for 48 hours. Helicopters with the rescue teams onboard were unable to reach the crash site due to intense heavy machine gun fire.

The second pilot lost during the first 378th OShAP personnel rotation was reported on 22 July 1985. 2nd AE pilot 1Lt Sergey Shumikhin failed to pull up from a dive for unknown reasons while performing his 11th attacking pass on the target. As with the previous loss, the pilot made no attempt at ejection, indicating that he had either been incapacitated or lost control of his jet during the attack.

SECOND ROTATION IN-THEATRE

The second personnel rotation, which arrived on 12 October 1985, consisted of air- and groundcrews drawn from 90th OShAP at Artsiz, under the command of Lt Col Alexander Rutskoy. The newly arriving pilots spent a few days flying with their combat-hardened predecessors to gain basic familiarisation with the demanding conditions in-theatre, before commencing independent combat operations on 21 October.

In February 1986 the regiment's structure was expanded to include one additional component squadron, with personnel drawn from 80th OShAP at Sital-Chai and commanded by Maj Sergey Komarov. The squadron numbering system within 378th OShAP had also been changed, as two of its component squadrons (1st and 2nd AE) and the command section remained based at Bagram, while the third squadron (3rd AE) was stationed at Kandahar, where it received eight new 7th Series aircraft and four 6th Series jets taken from the fleet of 2nd AE. Following this reorganisation, each of the three squadrons in Afghanistan was equipped with 12 Su-25s, with the remaining four being assigned to the regiment's command flight. In August 1986 four brand-new 8th Series 'Frogfoots' were taken on strength at Bagram as attrition replacements.

A welcome addition to the Su-25's arsenal during the second rotation period was the introduction of the Kh-25ML and Kh-29L laser-guided missiles, enabling stand-off strikes against high-value point targets. The first such missions were flown in April 1986 by 378th OShAP's CO, Lt Col Rutskoy, and 2nd AE CO, Maj Visotskiy. The pair used the new missiles, equipped with concrete-piercing/blast warheads, to seal the entrances of a number of caves used as personnel shelters and weapons/ammunition depots within the confines of the well-defended Zhawar (Djavara) 'superbase' complex near the city of Khost, west of the Afghanistan–Pakistan border.

A solitary Su-25 in 378th OShAP was specially configured for accurate bomb dropping, being equipped with finely tuned ASP-17BTs-8 electro-optical sights and employing Kh-29L and Kh-25ML laser-guided missiles that used the jet's Klyon-PS laser designator/rangefinder equipment for target designation. The previous use of non-tuned laser designator/rangefinders had resulted in misses of between 10 and 30 ft, which was deemed unacceptable when firing laser-guided missiles against point targets.

The Kh-29L laser-guided missile, fitted with a 755-lb shaped-charge warhead, was used for the first time by Soviet Su-25s in Afghanistan in April 1986 (*Author's collection*)

During guided missile launches using self-lasing, the hit accuracy came in for criticism because of laser-beam stability problems that afflicted the manually controlled laser designator/rangefinder equipment in the Su-25. The maximum target detection range was up to 4.94 miles in textbook conditions, while the minimum launch range was 1.84 miles. According to data released by Sukhoi, as many as 139 laser-guided missiles were launched by 378th OShAP Su-25s during the war in Afghanistan, using self-lasing or a BOMAN vehicle for external target designation – 137 rounds were reported to have hit their targets.

External lasing significantly improved aiming conditions for guided missiles, as Su-25 pilots were now free to commence defensive manoeuvring immediately after launching their weapons. Consequently, in 1987, a self-propelled laser-designation vehicle codenamed BOMAN was introduced into service by 378th OShAP. A makeshift targeting system, it was based on the body of a BTR-80 APC, equipped with a Klyon-PS system scavenged from an Su-25 that had been damaged beyond repair. Installed on a non-retractable support protruding above the body, the Klyon-PS was optically aimed at the target using the sight from a 12.7 mm machine gun. The BOMAN proved to be a highly effective and stable laser designation system. Whenever conditions permitted, it approached as close as possible to the target to create a powerful and stable laser spot, detected by the missile's seeker head at extended distances. This in turn allowed the 'Frogfoot' pilot to stay out range of enemy AAA and SAMs.

NOCTURNAL STRIKES

In 1986 the Su-25s began flying night combat sorties as a matter of routine. The nocturnal strikes necessitated the employment of SAB-100 and SAB-250 illumination bombs, carried by one of the jets in a four-aircraft flight. After dropping a string of illumination bombs, which descended slowly under parachutes, the remaining three Su-25s of the group pounded the targets that were now rendered visible with bombs and rockets, rolling in beneath the illumination bombs and using a shallow diving attack profile.

Between 12 October 1985 and 17 October 1986 the second personnel rotation of 378th OShAP flew no fewer than 15,620 combat sorties (including those logged by 3rd AE at Kandahar between February and October 1986), 2510 of which were flown at night. The total number of pre-planned strike missions was 5343 (about 34 per cent of the total). Each pilot from 1st and 2nd AEs logged between 270 and 300 combat hours, while individual 'Frogfoots' in-theatre completed between 250 and 300 sorties, averaging 224 flight hours. The Su-25s suffered 72 instances of in-flight combat damage, 54 being caused by small arms and heavy machine gun/AAA projectiles and

A group of 1st AE pilots from the second 378th OShAP rotation, which was in Afghanistan from October 1985 to October 1986. First on the left is 1Lt Vladislav Goncharenko and third from the left is 1Lt Sergey Gritskevich (*Author's collection – Aviatsia i Kosmonavtika*)

18 by SAM warhead fragments. Four aircraft were reported either lost or damaged beyond economical repair during emergency landings, and one pilot was killed in action.

The first Su-25 shot down during this rotation was the aircraft flown by the regimental CO himself, Lt Col Rutskoy. On 6 April 1986, during a low-level attack against the well-defended Zhawar *Mujahedeen* re-supply complex by a formation of four Su-25s, Rutskoy's aircraft was gunned down during his second attack pass by the combined fire of a shoulder-launched missile (possible a General Dynamics FIM-43 Redeye or Strela-2M) and AAA. Rutskoy, who flew a camera-equipped Su-25 for post-strike reconnaissance, ejected at an altitude of 820 ft at a high angle of bank. As a result of the latter, he sustained serious back injuries and a broken arm upon landing.

On a few occasions pilots flying Su-25s that had been badly damaged by SAMs elected to make emergency landings instead of ejecting over hostile territory. On 18 April 1986, for example, the jet of Maj Konstantin Ossipov, who was leading a four-aircraft formation, was hit by a SAM during the pilot's second attacking pass against a *Mujahedeen* stronghold within the notorious Zhawar complex. The punctured oil tank of the starboard engine caused a severe fire inside the fuselage that damaged the electrical system and knocked out most of the instruments in the cockpit. Realising that it would be impossible to return to Bagram, Ossipov decided to attempt an emergency landing at the nearby landing strip at Khost – despite having received orders from the ground to eject. To make matters worse, his aircraft was still carrying an ODAB-500P fuel-air bomb that been impossible to jettison due to the failed electrics.

Shortly before landing the Su-25's control runs failed, having been fully consumed by the severe fire raging on board. Maj Ossipov's luck held, however, as his aircraft continued descending and he eventually landed. He had touched down with sufficient force to destroy the undercarriage, the damaged Su-25 veering off the runway and colliding with a cow before it eventually stopped in a rice field. The damage caused by the SAM hit, the subsequent fire and the hard landing rendered the 'Frogfoot' beyond economical repair, so after the removal of all salvageable parts the aircraft was destroyed *in situ* with explosive charges.

The third Su-25 lost during this rotation was flown by Capt Alexander Smirnov of 1st AE, the aircraft being hit by a SAM while attacking the large Kokari-Sharshari re-supply complex close to the border with Iran on 23 August 1986. The jet caught fire, which destroyed the control runs, and the pilot was forced to bail out of his unflyable machine. After an uneventful descent, Capt Smirnov was promptly recovered by a C-SAR Mi-8MT helicopter loitering in the combat zone.

The fourth Su-25 write-off, and the only pilot loss during the second rotation, happened on 2 October 1986 when 1Lt Alexander Baranov of 2nd AE disappeared without trace, along with his jet, while conducting a night search-and-destroy single-aircraft mission from Bagram. He was instructed to follow a familiar Su-25 patrol route stretching from Bagram to Kabul and then turn south and fly along the Pakistani border in search of *Mujahedeen* activity – typically vehicles in re-supply convoys travelling with their headlights on. An intensive four-day search for the missing pilot and his aircraft proved fruitless.

During the second personnel rotation period (between October 1985 and October 1986) of 378th OShAP, 1Lt Vladislav Goncharenko received the highest national award, the Golden Star of Hero of Soviet Union, for his outstanding combat achievements. With 415 combat sorties to his credit totalling 360 hours, he served as a flight commander with 1st AE at Bagram, and later continued to serve as an instructor with 372nd OIShAE at Djizak, training inexperienced Su-25 pilots prior them being sent into combat in Afghanistan (*Author's collection – Aviatsia i Kosmonavtika*)

STRENGTHENED AIR DEFENCES

In 1985 *Mujahedeen* Oerlikon 20 mm AAA pieces and 12.7 mm and 14.5 mm heavy machine guns accounted for between 25 and 42 per cent of all downed Soviet aircraft. The effective range of the DShK-12.5 heavy machine gun was 5000 to 6000 ft, while the 20 mm AAA pieces remained effective well in excess of 6560 ft. By 1986 Soviet military intelligence estimated that the *Mujahedeen* had an inventory of no fewer than 530 heavy machine guns and 150 Oerlikons.

In 1982 Soviet forces first reported capturing shoulder-launched SAMs in the form of the Strela-2M, and their first successful employment by the *Mujahedeen* was reported the following year. In 1984 62 SAM launches were said to have been made by the *Mujahedeen*; this figure increased to 147 in 1985 and 847 in 1986, when no fewer than 23 Soviet fixed- and rotary-winged aircraft were downed by such weapons.

During a large-scale operation near Khost in March-April 1986, Sergey Gritskevich (a pilot from the 1985-86 Su-25 rotation) recalled that FACs on the ground counted as many as 60 SAM launches against attacking 'Frogfoots'. It later transpired, however, that the majority of these weapons had been unguided rocket-propelled grenades fired by RPG-7 launchers. The grenades left distinctive smoke trails in their wake before exploding in mid-air following the triggering of a self-destruction timer. They created a small smoke cloud upon detonation.

Protection against the *Mujahedeen's* heat-seeking missiles, introduced *en masse* during 1985-86, was initially provided by four ASO-2V-01 flare dispensers installed either side of the Su-25's fin. These ejected PPI-26 heat-emitting flares to decoy the missiles, the SAMs' heat-seeking guidance systems being known to be prone to high-temperature-flare jamming. However, these dispensers could not provide prolonged protection during multiple attacks because they contained only 126 flares. Prompt measures to enhance the Su-25's self-protection against heat-seeking SAMs were taken by attaching four additional ASO-2V-01 dispensers on the upper side of the engine nacelles, increasing flare capacity from 126 to 256, while the flare ejection controls were moved onto the pilot's control column. The battery of eight 32-round dispensers enabled the Su-25 to mount as many as eight attacking passes by 'pumping' flares non-stop in pre-set sequences. The first 378th OShAP 'Frogfoots' to have an increased number of ASO-2V dispensers and automatic flare-launch programming were modified on-site in Afghanistan in early 1986.

The increased SAM and AAA threat also meant that Su-25 pilots landing at Bagram now had to adopt a steep approach so as to stay within the guarded perimeter around the airfield as much as possible. Starting at an altitude of between 7900 ft and 9200 ft directly over the runway, pilots

A bird's-eye view of Kandahar airport in 1988. This was the permanent base of 3rd AE from February 1986 to July 1988 (*Author's collection*)

More than half of the grand total of about 60,000 combat sorties flown by the VVS in Afghanistan were performed at high altitude to avoid ground fire. Following the introduction of the Stinger missile in late 1986 the SAM threat effectively forced low-level attack aircraft out of their natural environment – the 'Frogfoot' was the VVS's most effective tool for CAS for ground forces. Here, 7th or 8th Series machine '22' flies over a typical mountain landscape during the first half of 1987 (*Author's collection – Aviatsia i Kosmonavtika*)

would enter into a steep spiral with a high rate of descent. Despite the strict implementation of these defensive measures, on 21 January 1987 1Lt Konstantin Pavlykov was shot down while in a left-hand turn towards Kabul immediately after taking off from Bagram. All subsequent takeoffs and landings were covered by pairs of Mi-24 patrolling non-stop around the airfield, their crews on the lookout for suspicious activity in an effort to prevent SAM launches from the *Mujahedeen*-controlled green zone next to the heavily guarded base perimeter.

In late 1986/early 1987, owing to the sharp increase in losses and heavy damage following the mass deployment of the new and much more lethal General Dynamics FIM-92 Stinger SAM, a set of new recommendations was issued in an effort to reduce the vulnerability of the attack aircraft. For instance, strikes now had to be mounted in sections of four to eight Su-25s, the four-aircraft group being preferred whenever possible.

Pilots were also advised to proceed to the target area at between 19,700 ft and 21,300 ft, after which attack runs were to be undertaken singly, with 15-second intervals between the aircraft. Only one run was to be made, rolling in to attack directly (i.e. without previously orbiting over the target) from the direction of the sun wherever possible. The attack runs of the succeeding aircraft in the group had to be conducted from different directions, with offsets of 15 to 20 degrees between the attack headings. Attack runs had to be made in a 45- to 60-degree dive, and in manual sighting mode only. Bombs were to be dropped at between 19,700 ft and 13,100 ft above the ground, with a hard deck (i.e. the minimum altitude at the lowest point of the dive, when the pilot levelled off, before starting the climb-out) limit set at 11,480 ft. Upon the release of ordnance, flares had to be pumped out until a height of 19,700 ft was attained. Upon initiating pull-out, a climb angle of between 25 and 30 degrees was recommended. Whilst climbing for height the aircraft was to fly in a zig-zag pattern, the pilot yanking 45 degrees left and right while rolling through 50 to 60 degrees.

With an increased number of Stinger SAMs and 20 mm AAA pieces in-theatre during the second half of 1986, all pre-planned strikes were now to be performed in a single attacking pass. However, re-supply convoys or targets designated by FACs during CAS missions still had to be attacked three or four times in a series of increasingly risky low-altitude passes in order to achieve the desired effect.

In July 1986 3rd AE was tasked with supporting a large-scale combined-arms operation aimed at destroying a number of enemy groups hiding in

After his Su-25 was hit by a SAM immediately after takeoff from Bagram on 21 January 1987, 1Lt Konstantin Pavlykov ejected and was killed in action in the Charikar area. He was posthumously awarded the Golden Star of Hero of the Soviet Union (*Author's collection*)

the green zone south of Kandahar. The Su-25s provided CAS for the ground forces, logging between 30 and 40 combat sorties each day. However, the operation took longer than expected owing to the fierce resistance of *Mujahedeen* fighters deeply entrenched in the green zone, and as a result the Soviet troops began to suffer painful losses. The enemy was able to hold its positions inside the green zone thanks to the uninterrupted supply of ammunition and reinforcements coming in from nearby Pakistan. Keen to bring an end to the offensive, and thus prevent further losses, the 40th Army's commanding officer tasked the most experienced pilots from the Kandahar-based 'Frogfoot' squadron with the job of laying minefields on 12 suspected routes used by the enemy re-supply convoys heading to the battle zone at night.

1Lt Alexander Koshkin, 3rd AE Deputy CO (Political Affairs), was among the small group of Su-25 pilots who conducted aerial mine-laying missions with KMGU-2 mine-dispersing pods. Mine-sowing passes were to be flown at speeds of between 340 mph and 435 mph at altitudes of between 660 ft and 1312 ft. The aircraft had to maintain straight and level flight for up to 12 seconds on each pass, followed by a U-turn, before starting another mine-laying leg. This made the Su-25s easy targets for enemy heavy machine guns, AAA and SAMs. Koshkin described how he managed to increase his chances of survival while performing these hazardous missions;

'In order to reduce the aircraft's vulnerability from ground fire during the multiple low-altitude legs I decided to fly under the cover of darkness, with the target area lit by strings of illumination bombs. The enemy routes were situated within a plain area adjacent to the Arganab River, allowing safe low-altitude nocturnal flying. I did some mission calculations, showing that a string of illumination bombs dropped by my wingman, Rustam Zagretidinov, would provide just enough light for me to fly two legs – using this method, in one sortie I was able to lay mines on four roads in the desert. I was opposed by fierce enemy fire, with the skies being lit up by the multiple tracers. The enemy gunners targeted the illumination bombs while I was working overhead and invisible to them. The enemy could hear my low-flying jet but were unable to see it. I had to be careful not to collide with the hilly terrain while I looked for the roads that needed to be mined, while at the same time avoiding being fired at from the ground.'

HEAVY LOSSES FOR THIRD ROTATION

The third personnel rotation with 1st and 2nd AEs of 378th OShAP took place between October 1986 and October 1987, and it involved pilots drawn from all three existing VVS Su-25-equipped frontline attack regiments at the time – 80th, 90th and 368th OShAPs.

The third rotation was deployed to Afghanistan just in time to face a new and far more lethal threat, as the *Mujahedeen* had begun deploying modern FIM-92A Stinger shoulder-launched SAMs (used for the first time in-theatre in September 1986). In addition to having vastly improved resistance to flare jamming, precision infrared homing, a more powerful warhead and a proximity fuse for increased kill probability, the Stinger could also hit targets at altitudes up to 14,800 ft. Between November 1986 and February 1987 no fewer than four Su-25s were gunned down using this deadly weapon, its mass introduction becoming a decisive factor in the conflict as it enabled *Mujahedeen* field commanders to effectively counter the threat posed by low-flying VVS helicopters and ground attack jets. The Stinger threat eventually forced the latter to deliver their ordnance from much higher altitudes, which immediately reduced their CAS effectiveness.

As a result of the introduction of the Stinger the third personnel rotation of 378th OShAP reported the highest combat attrition rate of the campaign, losing no fewer than 11 Su-25s and five pilots. An additional 'Frogfoot' was damaged beyond economical repair and returned to the Soviet Union for detailed combat damage analyses. Thus, the 40-aircraft 378th OShAP effectively lost 30 per cent of its fleet in only one year of intense COIN combat operations against an omnipresent, well-armed and motivated enemy. The heaviest losses were sustained by 2nd AE, accounting for three pilots and five aircraft, while 1st AE lost two pilots and four aircraft, 3rd AE two aircraft and the regimental command section reported one aircraft lost. In addition, another jet flown by a 1st AE pilot was withdrawn from use after taking a missile hit that inflicted serious damage, although its pilot managed to make a successful emergency landing.

This memorial to the five 378th OShAP pilots killed in action flying from Bagram between October 1986 and November 1987 was erected at the airfield in late 1987. The five pilots were, from left to right, 1Lt Igor Alyoshin, Capt Miroslav Burak and 1Lts Konstantin Pavlykov, Vladimir Paltusov and Viktor Zemlyakov. The memorial, minus the plaques, is still in existence at Bagram today (*Andrey Kozhemyakin archive via Author*)

According to accounts from former pilots of 378th OShAP who served with the third rotation, one of the downed Su-25s (flown by Capt Miroslav Burak) is believed to have taken a direct hit from a 122 mm illumination round fired by a Soviet field artillery unit overhead *Mujahedeen* positions being attacked by 'Frogfoots' at night on 5 February 1987. The aircraft, which happened to be in the wrong place at the wrong time, disintegrated in the mid-air, killing Burak.

Despite the proliferation of Stinger SAMs, only one Su-25 pilot was killed by enemy fire. Accidents caused by handling errors claimed the lives of Lt Igor Alyoshin on 20 November 1986 and 1Lt Victor Zemlyakov on 13 September 1987, while the loss of the fifth pilot, 1Lt Vladimir Paltusov on 20 July 1987, was attributed to the failure of the Su-25's oxygen equipment during high-altitude flight.

As previously noted in this chapter, 1Lt Konstantin Pavlykov became the sole fatality when his aircraft was brought down by a Stinger on 21 January 1987. Flying his third combat sortie of the day as a wingman, Pavlykov and his flight lead were tasked with covering transport and passenger aircraft taking off and landing at Kabul airport by dropping illumination bombs to fool heat-seeking missiles. Just moments after taking off from Bagram he was shot down, his aircraft being in a left turn when the Stinger hit it. Pavlykov ejected successfully but was then killed on the ground during a fierce and protracted firefight with a *Mujahedeen* group in the Charikar area. The C-SAR operation, launched several minutes after the shoot-down was reported, failed to locate the downed

8th Series Su-25 c/n 08033, flown by Maj Anatoliy Obedkov, was one of the most seriously battle-damaged 'Frogfoots' that a pilot managed to land. Exploding in close proximity to Obedkov's aircraft, the Stinger warhead created a hole three feet high and five feet long on the starboard side, causing instant engine failure and a starting a fire inside the fuselage, fed by hydraulic fluid leaking under pressure. This in turn consumed 95 per cent of the titanium control rod diameter. Fortunately, the control system remained functional until the end of this very dramatic sortie (*Sukhoi Company*)

pilot in time, and after dark the effort was terminated owing to the increased threat level.

For his outstanding war achievements and determined resistance after ejection, 1Lt Pavlykov was posthumously awarded the Golden Star of Hero of the Soviet Union. The report listing his combat achievements noted that between late October 1986 and 21 January 1987 Pavlykov had flown 89 combat sorties, and his exploits included the destruction/neutralisation of seven heavy machine gun nests, four AAA pieces, six recoilless artillery teams, four weapons/munitions storage depots, 17 motor vehicles and up to 120 enemy combatants.

The third rotation of 378th OShAP, which had taken place between 24 October 1986 and 20 October 1987, amassed 12,269 combat sorties totalling 9317 flying hours. Of these, 1119 sorties (8.6 per cent of the total) were dedicated to CAS, 6809 (59.4 per cent) to pre-planned strikes, 338 (2.8 per cent) to aerial reconnaissance and 432 (3.5 per cent) to aerial mine-laying. As many as 41,349 rockets and 26,878 bombs were expended, as well as 1992 miscellaneous bombs (mainly of illumination type).

SURVIVING HITS

Maj Anatoliy Obedkov, Chief of Staff of 1st AE, was one of three pilots who made emergency landings in their heavily damaged Su-25s after taking SAM hits. In Obedkov's case the missile damaged the fuselage and the starboard engine of his aircraft during a low-level re-supply convoy attack mission flown by an eight-aircraft formation in the Surubi Dam area on 28 July 1987. Obedkov recalled;

'The SAM detonated next to my starboard engine, shredding the nacelle and the upper part of the combustion chamber and jamming the low-pressure turbine. The fragments from the detonated warhead damaged both DC converters, and with the electrical system lost it proved impossible to jettison the bombs hanging under the wing. The only working instruments in the cockpit were the vertical speed indicator and the airspeed indicator.

'Furthermore, the ravaging fire that destroyed the DC converters caused the overheating of a wiring bundle next to them, resulting in a series of short circuits. These, in turn, led to the unintentional in-flight deployment of the aircraft's brake 'chute at a speed of around 220 mph, the 'chute failing to separate immediately after that. Luckily, it fell away a few seconds later. However, seeing a deployed 'chute falling to the ground, the remaining seven pilots in my group thought I had ejected. After separation, the twin-dome 'chute descended for 160 ft, and then both domes suddenly collapsed and fell to the ground. All of the pilots in the formation escorting me initially thought that I had been killed in my ejection attempt owing to the failure of the parachute.

'Somehow I managed to stay aloft and coax my damaged aeroplane to Kabul, where, because of severe buffeting, I decided to attempt a landing. Despite having damaged flight controls, I successfully touched down in the still burning jet. Without functioning brakes and a brake 'chute, I rolled along the entire length of the runway at high speed, overshot and continued on over the rough terrain until the aeroplane finally came to a halt in a trench next to a minefield.'

Obedkov's 8th Series Su-25 ('23', c/n 08033) had been hit by one of two Stingers launched by the targeted convoy's air defence section. In addition to the completely destroyed electrical system, the severe damage inflicted by the missile caused a complete failure of the aircraft's dual-redundant hydraulic system. The on-board fire was fed by flammable hydraulic fluid spraying under pressure from the severed control lines, and the control runs also suffered badly from heat damage. After the landing it was discovered that some 95 per cent of the titanium control rod diameter had been eaten away by the fire. Fortunately the control system remained functional until the end of this very dramatic sortie.

As Obedkov recalled later, after the hit his heavily laden 'Frogfoot', which was carrying two 800-litre external tanks (and 3000 litres of fuel internally), four RBK-250 250 kg (550-lb) cluster bombs and two full B8M rocket packs, remained airborne at a speed as low 105 mph. It gradually accelerated to 175 mph and even climbed despite having one inoperable engine. Following its recovering from the trench at Kabul, the aircraft was written-off. The Su-25 was subsequently handed over to Sukhoi so that it could undertake a detailed examination of the damage and evaluate the effectiveness of the self-protection features fitted to 8th Series 'Frogfoots'.

The first pilot from this rotation to suffer a SAM hit in his 'Frogfoot' and still manage a successful emergency landing was Maj Alexander Rybakov, Deputy CO (Political Affairs) of 2nd AE. On 28 May 1987 he was flying as wingman to his CO, Lt Col Grigoriy Strepetov, on a CAS mission for Soviet forces in the Alikheil area that were supporting Afghani troops involved in a firefight with a *Mujahedeen* group. During the Su-25s' second attacking pass the FAC on the ground spotted a SAM that had been launched at Rybakov's jet. He issued a prompt warning just as Rybakov started pulling away from the target area after he had completed his diving pass. With his aircraft flying relatively slowly as he tried to regain altitude, Rybakov was unable to make the sharp turns needed to evade the missile.

The SAM (some Russian sources claim that it was a Shorts Blowpipe, which was using manual command-to-line-of-sight guidance) detonated close to the aircraft and fragments punctured the canopy, inflicting superficial wounds on the pilot's face. Unperturbed, Rybakov requested permission to perform a third firing pass, but Strepetov ordered that he immediately return to base. Only then did Rybakov

Maj Alexander Rybakov, Deputy CO (Political Affairs) of 2nd AE, made a successful emergency landing on 28 May 1987 after his Su-25 suffered a SAM hit during a CAS mission. The port engine was damaged and shrapnel pierced the aircraft's skin and entered the cockpit, wounding the pilot in the face (*Author's collection – Aviatsia i Kosmonavtika*)

This 9th Series Su-25, '02', flown by Maj Alexander Rybakov, is seen resting on its belly after the pilot's emergency landing at Kabul on 28 May 1987, after taking a SAM hit. The aircraft is armed with two B8M rocket packs (*Author's collection*)

realise that his aircraft was more severely damaged than he had thought immediately after it was hit. The port engine began losing thrust, with the temperature going into the red sector. Upon entering clouds the jet lost speed, at which point Rybakov was forced to react promptly in order to prevent a stall from developing. The asymmetric thrust generated by the inoperable port engine caused the aircraft to turn to the left, but Rybakov was able to maintain control, establishing straight-and-level flight, regaining speed and eventually emerging from the cloud.

For his bravery in continuing to fly his heavily damaged aircraft, '47', and returning to base, 1Lt Pyotr Golubtsov, seen in the cockpit of his 7th Series Su-25, was awarded the Combat Red Star medal. A Stinger had exploded near the jet's tail section just as the pilot was about to attack enemy fighters in a suburb of Kandahar during a CAS mission for Special Forces on 24 October 1987 (*Sukhoi Company*)

The next step required him to turn towards the nearest airfield for an emergency landing. Guided by Strepetov, Rybakov managed to reach Kabul. By then, however, the Su-25 had already lost both of its hydraulic systems, and the undercarriage's emergency lowering system had also failed. The pilot decided not to try a gear-up landing on the paved runway, electing instead to use the earth strip alongside it. Touching down gently and sliding on its belly for more than 1300 ft, the badly damaged Su-25 eventually ground to halt in the soft earth.

A 3rd AE pilot, 1Lt Pyotr Golubtsov, suffered a Stinger hit in the tail that caused significant damage on 24 October 1987, although he managed to regain control of the aircraft and land safely. Golubtsov was flying at low level as a wingman for a pair of Su-25s tasked with providing CAS for Special Operations forces involved in a firefight with the enemy in a suburb of Kandahar when his aircraft was targeted. His 7th Series 'Frogfoot' ('47'), armed with six UB-32M rocket pods, was hit by a Stinger during the Su-25s' first low-level attack pass. The detonation of the SAM's warhead destroyed most of the jet's tail section behind the engine nozzles, inflicting heavy damage and causing subsequent failure of most of the aircraft's systems.

Nevertheless, the young Su-25 pilot remained cool and, escorted by his leader, Maj Sergey Gorohov, he eventually managed to land safely at Kandahar at twilight, although the aircraft veered off the runway and entered a minefield. After examining the extent of the combat damage inflicted on Golubtsov's aircraft, VVS command personnel initially decided to write it off. However, they later ordered it to be repaired *in situ* in an experimental programme aimed at evaluating the Su-25's reparability in field conditions.

A close up of the damage inflicted to 1Lt Pyotr Golubtsov's 3rd AE Su-25 '47' on 24 October 1987. The Stinger's warhead detonated close to the tail and destroyed most of the underfuselage section just behind the engine nozzles, but the 7th Series aircraft remained flyable and Golubtsov landed at Kandahar (*Sukhoi Company*)

EJECTIONS

During 378th OShAP's third rotation period as many as six pilots successfully ejected from their badly damaged 'Frogfoots' after taking SAM hits. The first pilot to abandon *(text continues on page 46)*

COLOUR PLATES

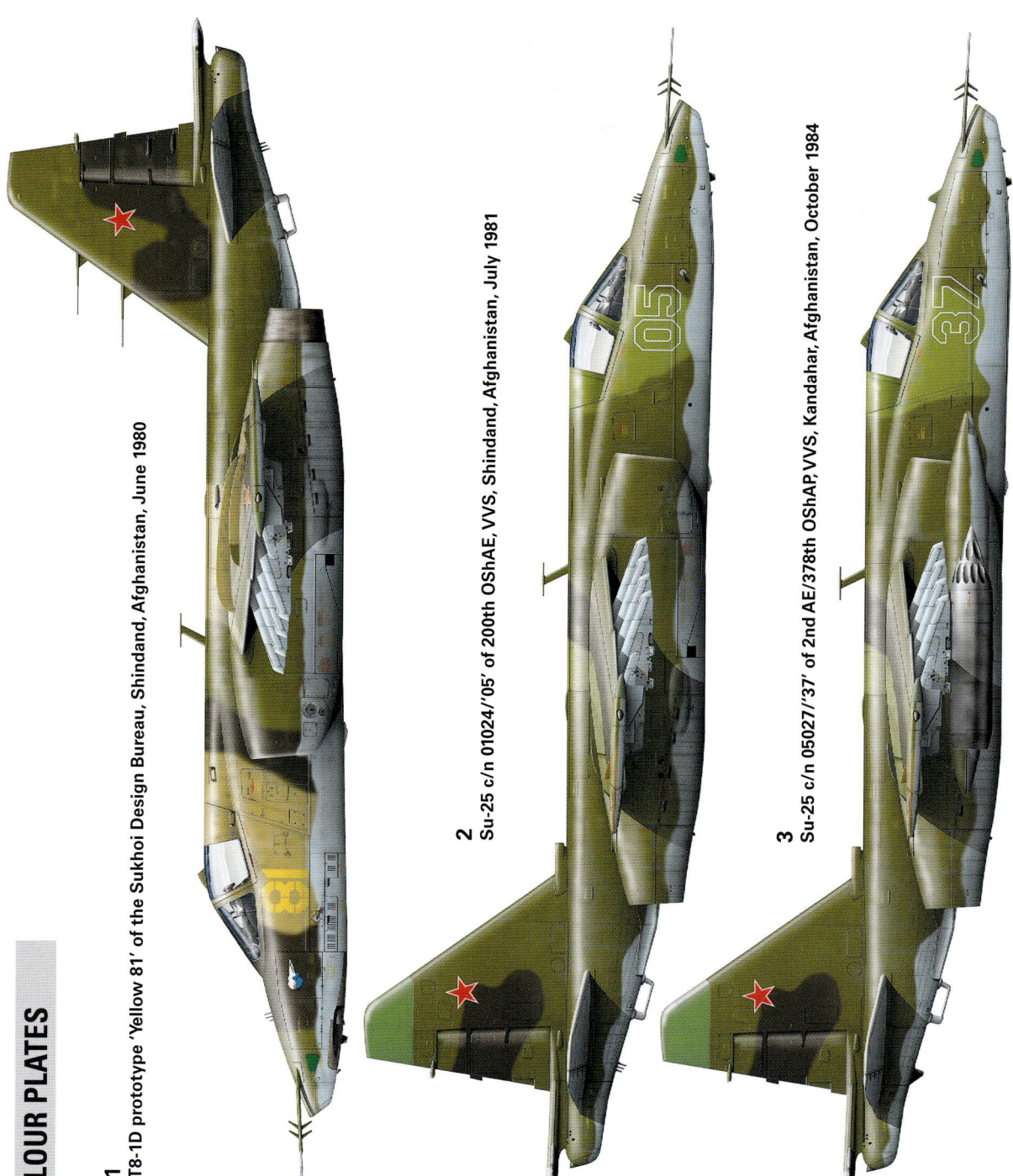

1
T8-1D prototype 'Yellow 81' of the Sukhoi Design Bureau, Shindand, Afghanistan, June 1980

2
Su-25 c/n 01024/'05' of 200th OShAE, VVS, Shindand, Afghanistan, July 1981

3
Su-25 c/n 05027/'37' of 2nd AE/378th OShAP, VVS, Kandahar, Afghanistan, October 1984

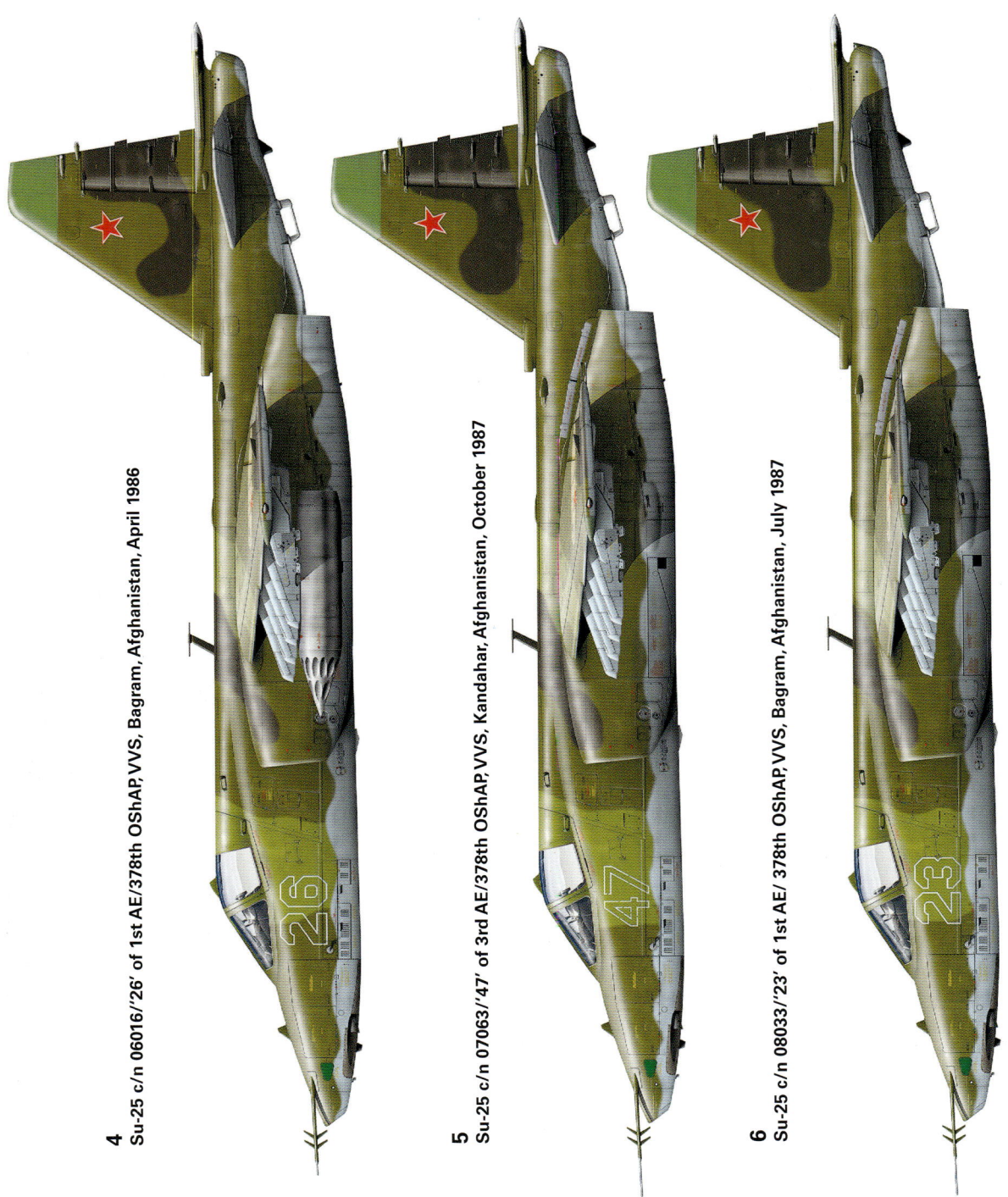

4
Su-25 c/n 06016/'26' of 1st AE/378th OShAP, VVS, Bagram, Afghanistan, April 1986

5
Su-25 c/n 07063/'47' of 3rd AE/378th OShAP, VVS, Kandahar, Afghanistan, October 1987

6
Su-25 c/n 08033/'23' of 1st AE/378th OShAP, VVS, Bagram, Afghanistan, July 1987

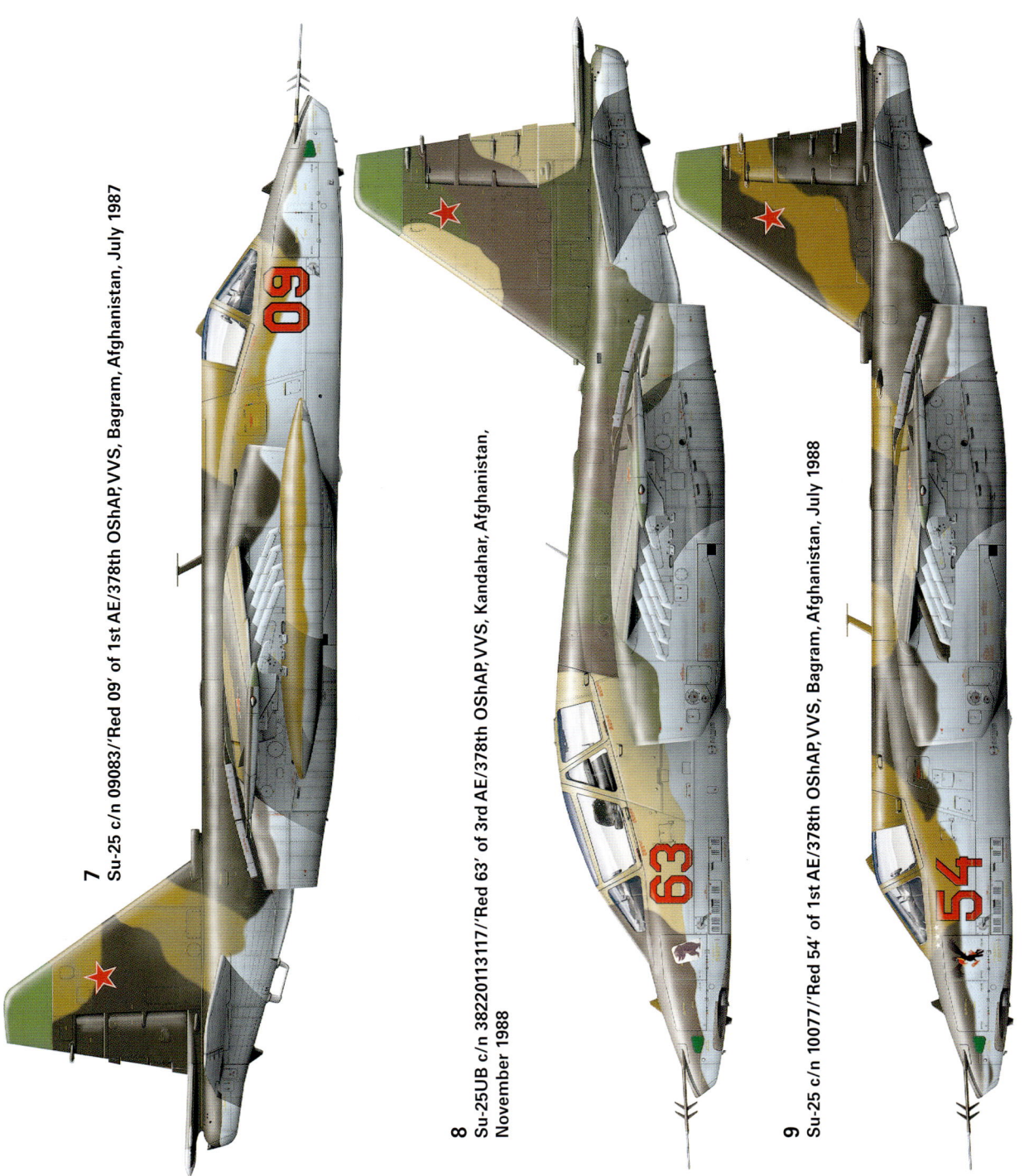

7
Su-25 c/n 09083/'Red 09' of 1st AE/378th OShAP, VVS, Bagram, Afghanistan, July 1987

8
Su-25UB c/n 38220113117/'Red 63' of 3rd AE/378th OShAP, VVS, Kandahar, Afghanistan, November 1988

9
Su-25 c/n 10077/'Red 54' of 1st AE/378th OShAP, VVS, Bagram, Afghanistan, July 1988

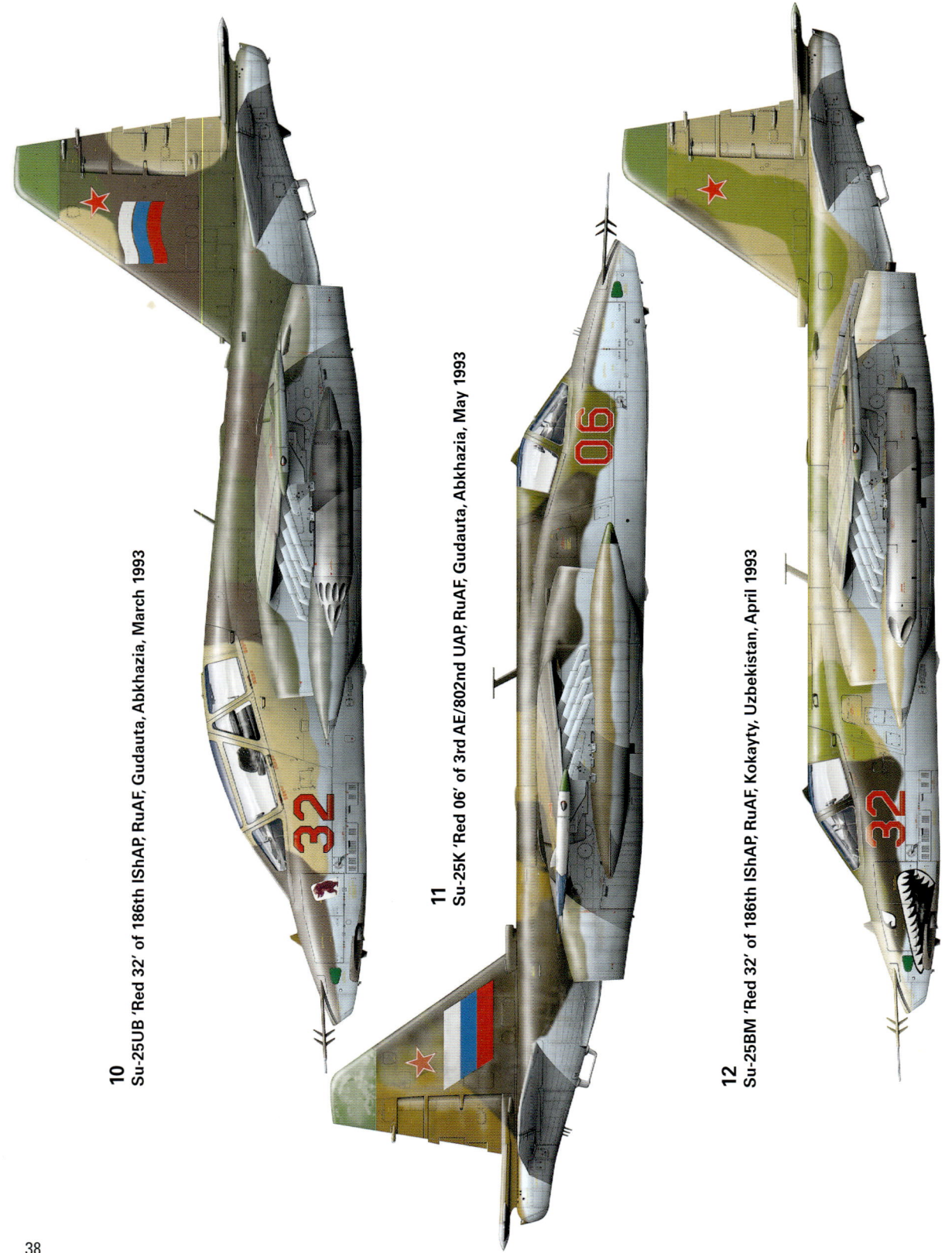

10
Su-25UB 'Red 32' of 186th IShAP, RuAF, Gudauta, Abkhazia, March 1993

11
Su-25K 'Red 06' of 3rd AE/802nd UAP, RuAF, Gudauta, Abkhazia, May 1993

12
Su-25BM 'Red 32' of 186th IShAP, RuAF, Kokayty, Uzbekistan, April 1993

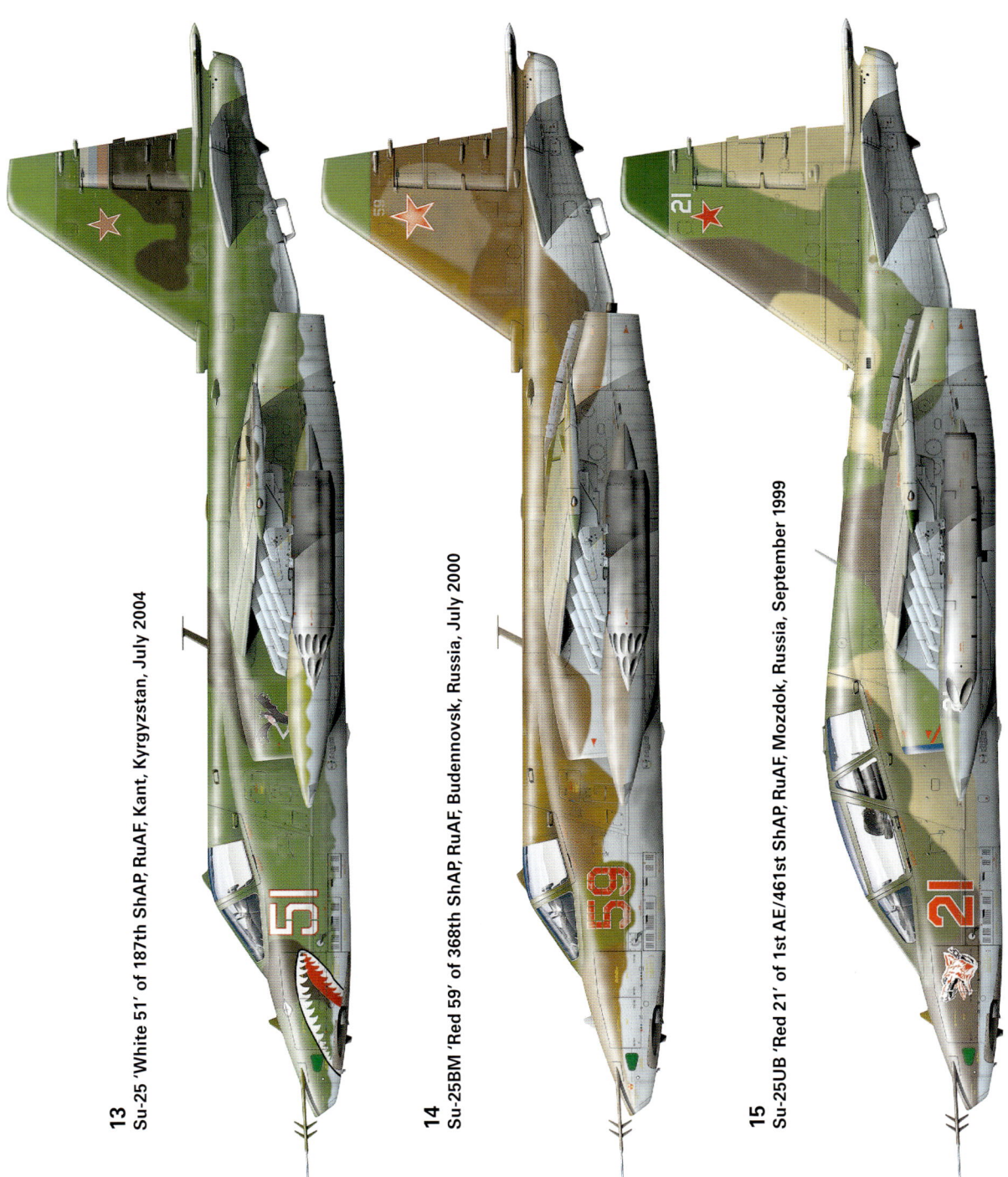

13
Su-25 'White 51' of 187th ShAP, RuAF, Kant, Kyrgyzstan, July 2004

14
Su-25BM 'Red 59' of 368th ShAP, RuAF, Budennovsk, Russia, July 2000

15
Su-25UB 'Red 21' of 1st AE/461st ShAP, RuAF, Mozdok, Russia, September 1999

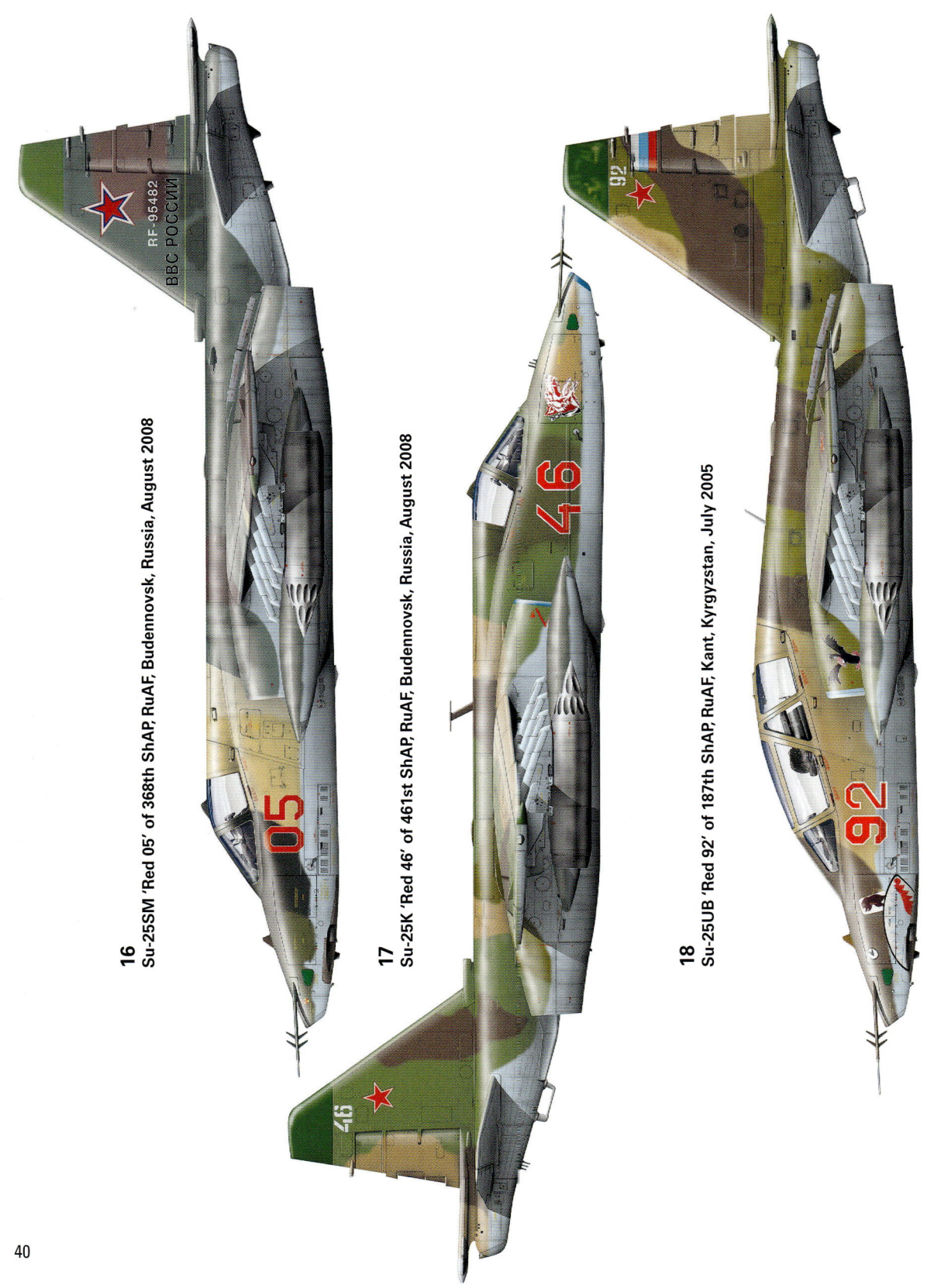

16
Su-25SM 'Red 05' of 368th ShAP, RuAF, Budennovsk, Russia, August 2008

17
Su-25K 'Red 46' of 461st ShAP, RuAF, Budennovsk, Russia, August 2008

18
Su-25UB 'Red 92' of 187th ShAP, RuAF, Kant, Kyrgyzstan, July 2005

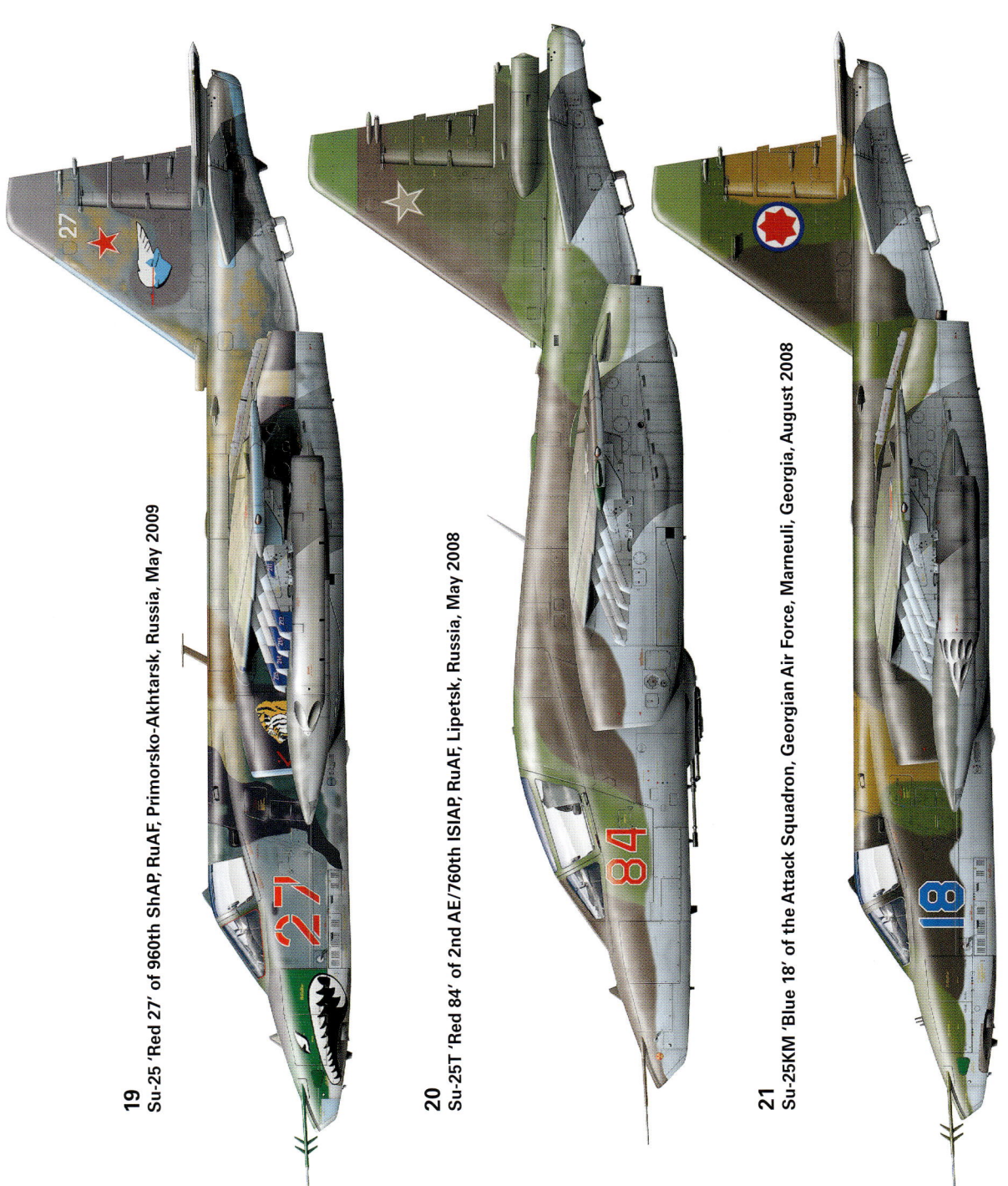

19
Su-25 'Red 27' of 960th ShAP, RuAF, Primorsko-Akhtarsk, Russia, May 2009

20
Su-25T 'Red 84' of 2nd AE/760th ISIAP, RuAF, Lipetsk, Russia, May 2008

21
Su-25KM 'Blue 18' of the Attack Squadron, Georgian Air Force, Marneuli, Georgia, August 2008

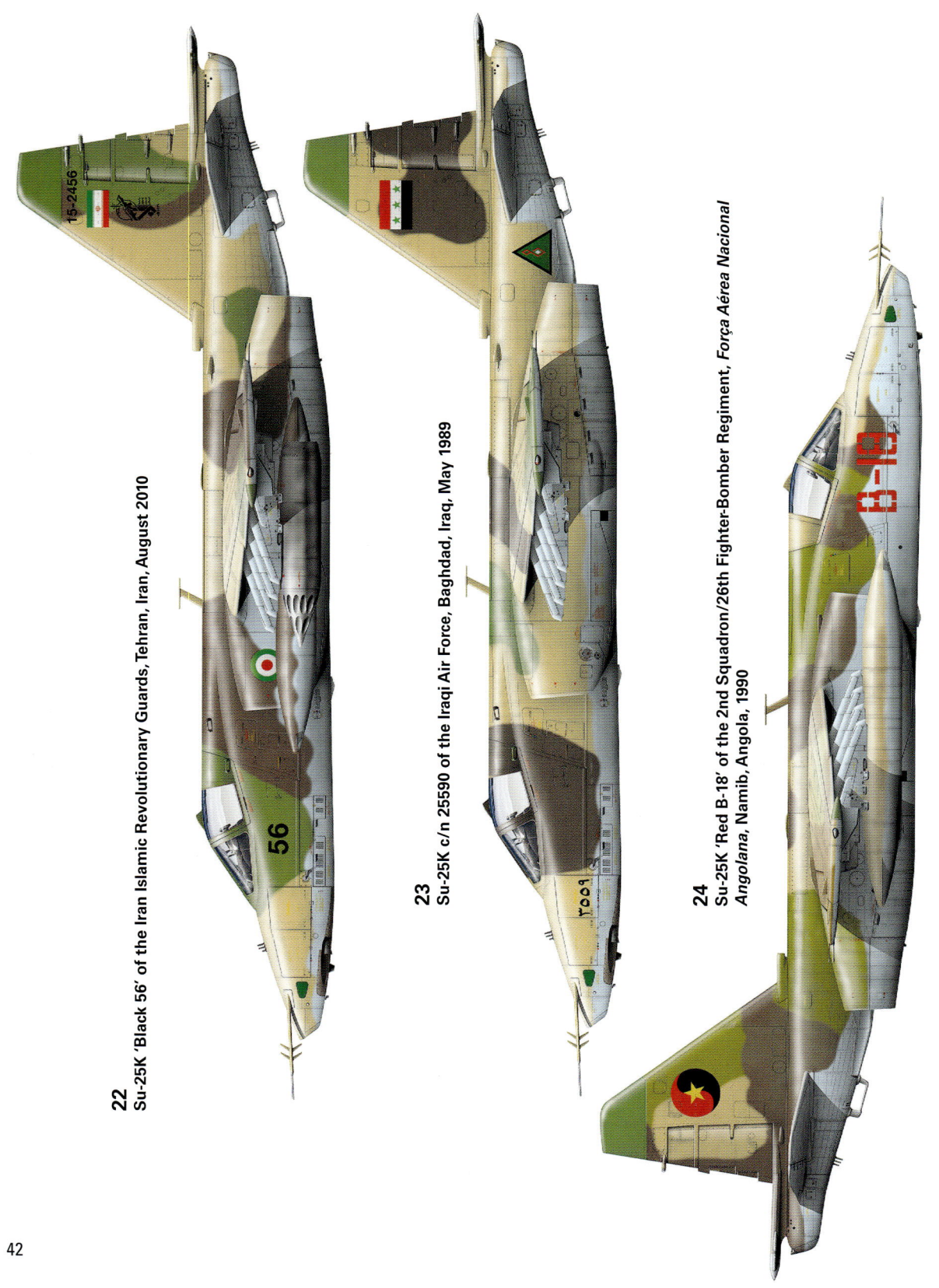

22
Su-25K 'Black 56' of the Iran Islamic Revolutionary Guards, Tehran, Iran, August 2010

23
Su-25K c/n 25590 of the Iraqi Air Force, Baghdad, Iraq, May 1989

24
Su-25K 'Red B-18' of the 2nd Squadron/26th Fighter-Bomber Regiment, *Força Aérea Nacional Angolana*, Namib, Angola, 1990

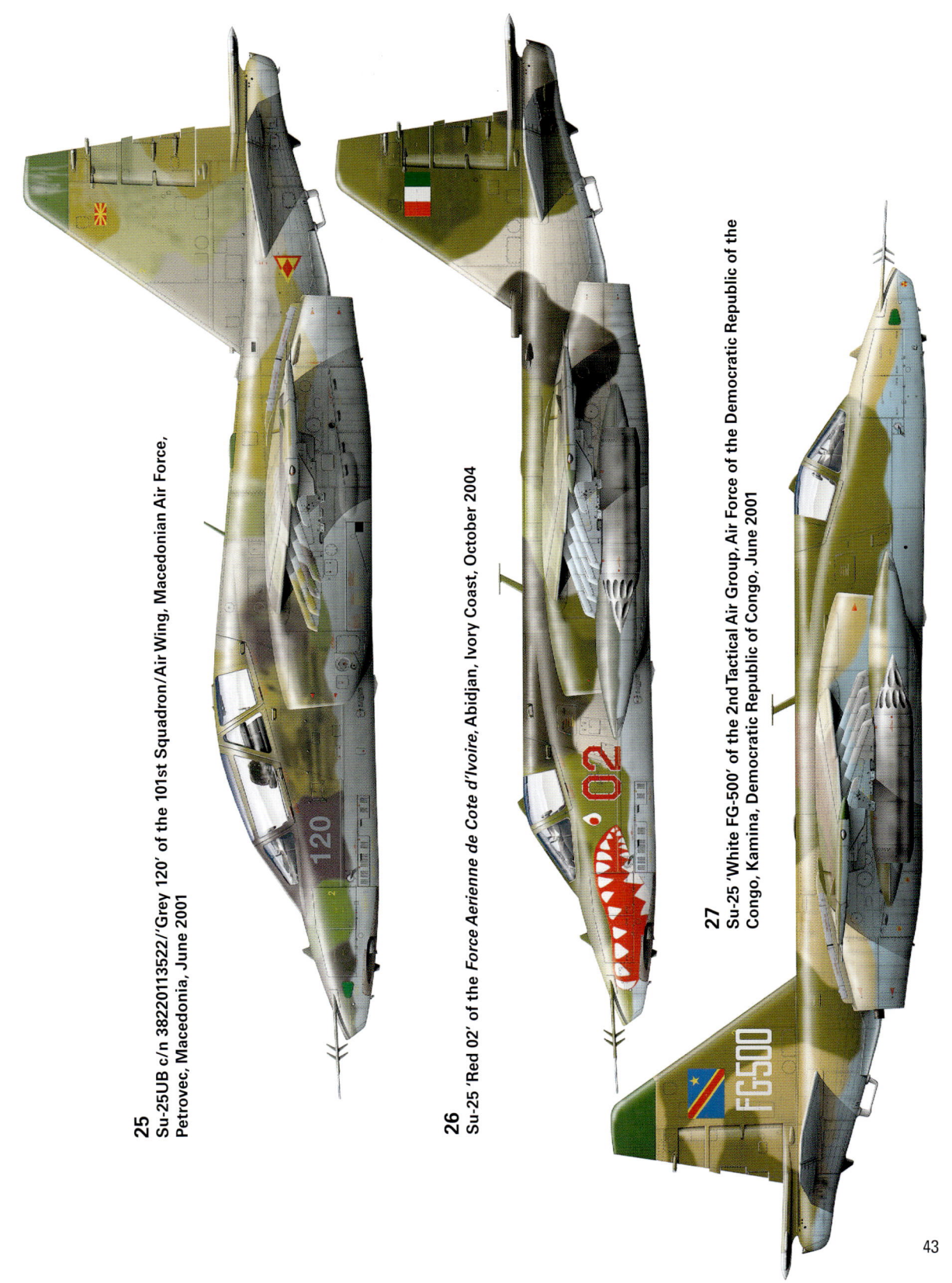

25
Su-25UB c/n 38220113522/'Grey 120' of the 101st Squadron/Air Wing, Macedonian Air Force, Petrovec, Macedonia, June 2001

26
Su-25 'Red 02' of the *Force Aerienne de Cote d'Ivoire*, Abidjan, Ivory Coast, October 2004

27
Su-25 'White FG-500' of the 2nd Tactical Air Group, Air Force of the Democratic Republic of the Congo, Kamina, Democratic Republic of Congo, June 2001

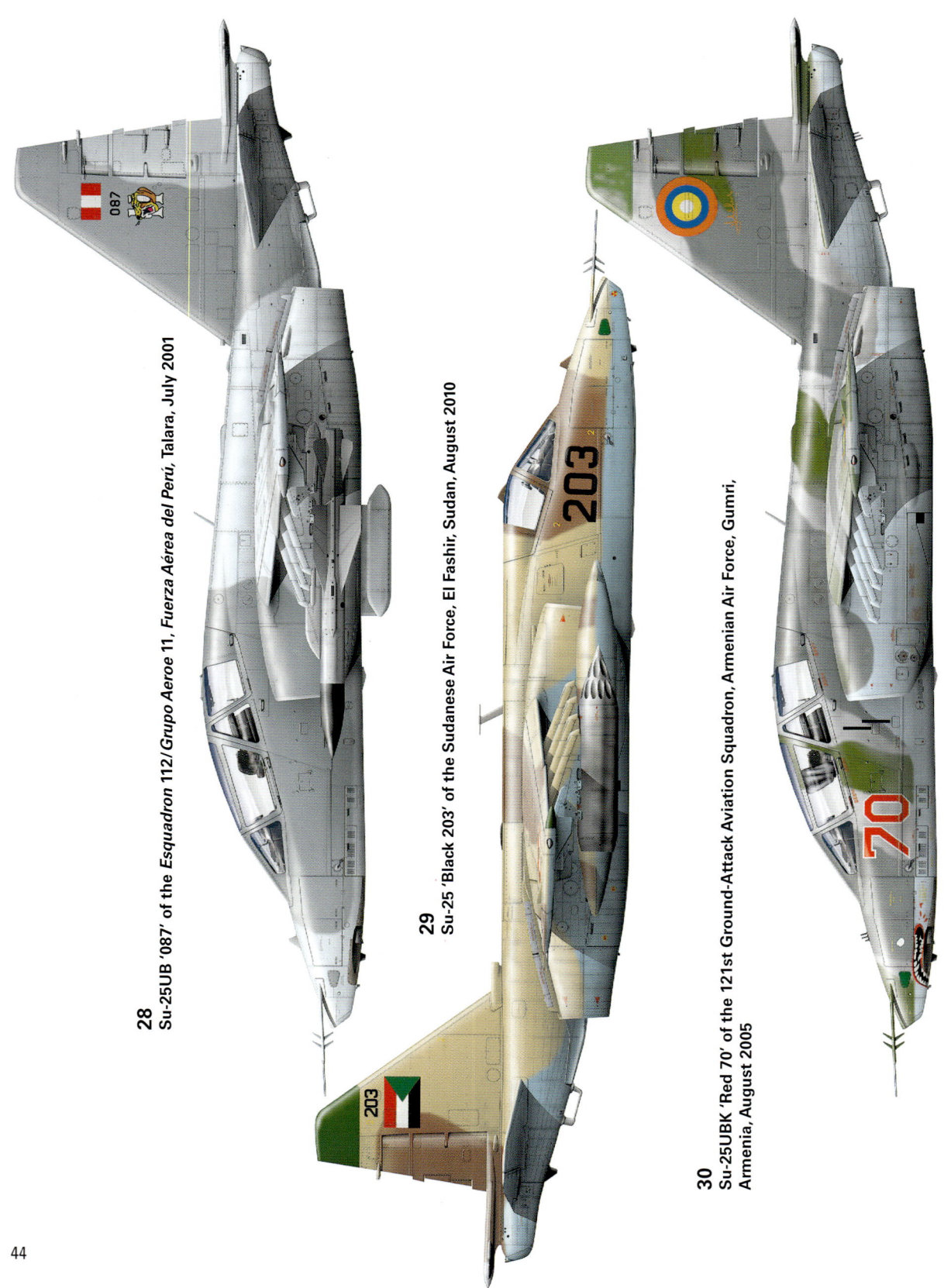

28
Su-25UB '087' of the Esquadron 112/Grupo Aeroe 11, *Fuerza Aérea del Perú*, Talara, July 2001

29
Su-25 'Black 203' of the Sudanese Air Force, El Fashir, Sudan, August 2010

30
Su-25UBK 'Red 70' of the 121st Ground-Attack Aviation Squadron, Armenian Air Force, Gumri, Armenia, August 2005

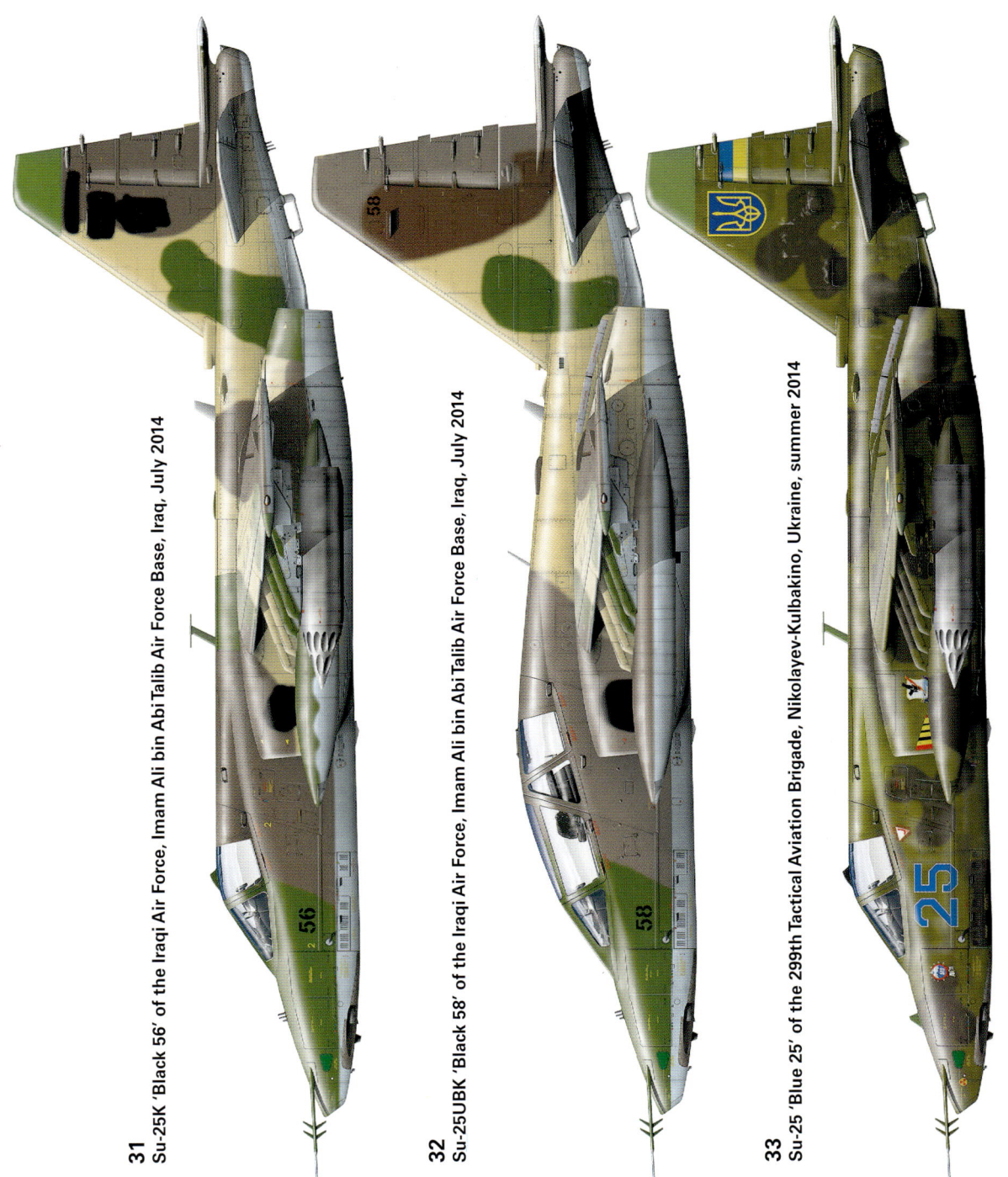

31
Su-25K 'Black 56' of the Iraqi Air Force, Imam Ali bin Abi Talib Air Force Base, Iraq, July 2014

32
Su-25UBK 'Black 58' of the Iraqi Air Force, Imam Ali bin Abi Talib Air Force Base, Iraq, July 2014

33
Su-25 'Blue 25' of the 299th Tactical Aviation Brigade, Nikolayev-Kulbakino, Ukraine, summer 2014

his terminally damaged Su-25 was Lt Col Nikolay Ploskonos, 1st AE CO, whose jet was hit by a Stinger on 18 November 1986 during his pull-out from a dive attack. He managed to eject successfully and was rescued by the C-SAR team despatched to recover him. Ploskonos' aircraft was almost certainly the first Su-25 to have been claimed by a Stinger in Afghanistan.

Alexander Koshkin, one of most combat-experienced pilots of 378th OShAP's 3rd AE, flew 515 combat sorties in Afghanistan between March 1986 and January 1987. One of his most memorable missions occurred on 3 December 1986 whilst he was temporarily assigned to 2nd AE to mentor the less experienced pilots in the unit. Two Su-25s were lost that day to Stinger SAMs while attacking targets in the same valley.

'I was on a revenge mission near the Surubi Dam, east of Kabul,' Koshkin recalled, 'pounding a valley next to a Kadashi village [15 miles east of Kabul]. An hour earlier one of our pilots, Capt Alexey Fabry, had taken a hit from a Stinger SAM [over Rayan village]. I was in the second four-aircraft formation heading to bomb the same target and never saw the hit. We were five minutes behind the first formation but heard everything on the radio – how he had reported the hit, how they shouted "eject", and how he had replied "I will try to reach Kabul". In the event Capt Fabry's luck held for he managed to reach the road leading to Kabul before ejecting from his now uncontrollable aircraft. He was recovered by friendly troops.'

After delivering their bombs on the target, the second flight turned back to Bagram and, following quick refuelling and rearming, two four-aircraft flights were despatched to the same valley to target the enemy fighters that had downed Capt Fabry.

'I memorised that valley, where I had spotted no fewer than ten heavy machine gun positions that needed to be suppressed before we started our attack runs. Before takeoff we had agreed with the other flight, led by Lt Col Grigoriy Strepetov, that they would take care of hitting the air defence positions before we targeted the valley. However, upon reaching the target area, Strepetov's flight headed for the wrong valley – they flew up a valley to the right rather than to the left. The four Su-25s quickly manoeuvred into a racetrack pattern over the wrong valley and commenced their attacks, which lasted for five minutes. After the flight had expended its ordnance Strepetov reported that the mission had been accomplished and he and his men were heading home.'

Su-25 '06' flies over a typical Afghanistan mountain landscape. This photograph was taken only days before this aircraft took a Stinger hit (*Andrey Kozhemyakin archive via Author*)

Moments later the leader of Koshkin's formation, Maj Shulimov, rolled in to attack and suppress the correct DShK heavy machine gun emplacements marked on the pilots' maps. He made two passes and then Koshkin and his wingman followed suit, rolling in and making four attacks each, dropping bombs and firing rockets. Once they had cleared the target area, the fourth Su-25 from the flight, flown by Maj Alexander Rybakov, rolled in to deliver its ordnance onto a valley floor already obscured by fire and smoke. After completing their work the Su-25s climbed away to 16,400 ft to form up into formation and return home.

Maj Shulimov, however, decided to mount one more attack, flying back into the valley to deliver his remaining ordnance. Pulling up in a westerly direction after his last run, he headed towards a high ridgeline rising above 16,400 ft. During the steep climb-out his speed dropped away, at which point a SAM was fired at him from the slope immediately beneath his slow-flying Su-25. Koshkin recalled this critical moment;

'The missile's trail looked like cigarette smoke. It hit the Su-25 accurately in the tail, tearing off skin panels, and then an explosion followed. I shouted, "Kolya, you took a missile hit! Eject!" Having realised what had happened he promptly ejected, leaving the aircraft to fly into the sloping mountain and hit it just beneath the top of the ridgeline. At that moment my knees began shaking because Shulimov had failed to pass over the ridgeline and reach neutral territory. Instead, my comrade found himself descending beneath his parachute inside the valley we had just bombed. I rolled in and attacked the site from where the SAM had been fired. It was not an act of revenge any more. Now I was just trying to keep the enemies' heads down, and to stop them from organising a search operation to capture the downed pilot.'

Koshkin immediately informed the C^2 Centre at Bagram about the location of the ejected pilot, who had landed in a valley with an elevation of 11,800 ft above sea level. The remaining two aircraft from the flight attacked the village and the adjacent road, but then had to turn back to Bagram after running out of ordnance. Koshkin continued circling overhead alone, however, keeping his eyes firmly fixed on the parachute canopy 'splashed' on the steep slope while he awaited the arrival of the C-SAR party. Although his aircraft had a low fuel state, he was the only one on-scene able to guide the helicopters directly to Shulimov's position, as the downed pilot's personal locator beacon, which was supposed to be activated automatically upon landing, remained silent.

When the C-SAR helicopters finally reached the scene Koshkin had considerable difficulty directing them to the right spot, as their crews were initially unable to detect the parachute canopy despite detailed instructions from the Su-25 pilot circling overhead. By then his remaining fuel was sufficient for only ten more minutes of flight, so after the helicopters made one more fruitless pass over the valley Koshkin was on the verge of having to head for Bagram. Finally, a flight technician in one the helicopters spotted the parachute canopy, and shortly thereafter his Mi-8MT landed at the site previously pinpointed by Koshkin. Upon touching down, a group of rescuers jumped from the helicopter and streaked downhill to recover Shulimov.

'I continued circling overhead to cover the group from possible attacks, remaining above the rescue scene until the helicopter took off. I tried not to look at the fuel gauge during this final phase of the rescue. I then began climbing up to 19,680 ft while turning towards Bagram. A few minutes later I made visual contact with the airfield and warned the C^2 Centre that I was going to perform a direct landing approach (i.e. without entering into the landing circuit). While on the glideslope the starboard engine flamed out because it had run out of fuel, and shortly afterwards the port one followed suit. I continued flying in a complete silence that

2nd AE's CO, Lt Col Grigoriy Strepetov, had a very difficult tour in Afghanistan between October 1986 and October 1987. His squadron lost three pilots and five aircraft in combat, most of them brought down by the newly introduced Stinger SAM (*Author's collection – Aviatsia i Kosmonavtika*)

I have never heard in flight before. The Su-25, however, is a good machine, with a large wingspan that allows gliding with engines off, so I eventually managed to reach the runway [after 15 seconds of un-powered flight] without further adventures.'

On 28 January 1987 an Su-25 flown by Maj Eduard Ryabov, Deputy CO of 2nd AE, was shot down in the Jalalabad area. The VVS's official magazine, *Aviatsia i Kosmonavtika*, published an article on the incident, stating that Ryabov was part of a four-aircraft formation that had been tasked with providing CAS for a tactical air assault party that was being inserted by helicopters. Ryabov was flying as wingman in the first pair when his Su-25 took a SAM hit whilst pulling out of a dive during his second attack pass. Struggling for both speed and altitude when targeted by the missile, Ryabov was 'too low and too slow' to initiate hard manoeuvring in order to avoid the SAM. The Stinger warhead detonated close to the aircraft's tail, knocking out both hydraulic systems as well as the DC generators, and then the engines lost thrust.

Ryabov had little choice but to eject, and he descended onto a sloping hill next to a village. After seeing their comrade eject, the remaining three Su-25 pilots, led by the CO of 2nd AE, Lt Col Grigoriy Strepetov, began circling over the ejection site, using their remaining rockets to see off a group of locals who were walking towards Ryabov. Immediately after descending and disconnecting his parachute harness, Ryabov began running uphill as far as possible from the village, while his comrades strove to stop or at least delay the advance of the locals with hostile intentions. The three Su-25s covering the ejected pilot soon ran out of fuel and ammunition and departed the area, but they were promptly replaced by another four-aircraft 'Frogfoot' formation that had been scrambled from Bagram to support the rescue effort. The newly arrived jets continued strafing the trail leading from the village to the top of the hill in an effort to delay the advance of the hostile locals.

Some 20 minutes after the ejection a C-SAR party of two Mi-8MTs approached the area. Upon hearing the helicopters Ryabov emerged from his hide and fired his only signal flare, which generated a highly visible orange smoke cloud. One of the helicopters turned towards the smoke, descended and hovered over the top of the hill while Ryabov quickly jumped on board.

On 2 April the 'Frogfoot' flown by 1Lt Andrey Garbuzov of 1st AE was hit by a SAM during a combat mission in the Alikheil area. The pilot ejected and was promptly recovered by a C-SAR team. Anatoliy Obedkov, who led the second four-aircraft group participating in this mission, stated that Garbuzov's aircraft had taken a hit from an air-to-air missile fired by a Pakistani Air Force (PAF) F-16A Fighting Falcon, although this was not confirmed by PAF sources. Obedkov noted that the Su-25 group was flying inside Pakistani airspace at the time the 'Frogfoot' was hit.

On 1 June 3rd AE pilot 1Lt Sergey Koinov ejected after taking a SAM hit near Kandahar airfield and was promptly recovered.

'FITTER' PILOT RESCUE

From time to time the Su-25s were also called upon to participate in C-SAR missions in high-threat areas. On 16 May 1987 Lt Col Grigoriy Strepetov, CO of 2nd AE, conducted such a mission, intended to rescue a pilot of 263rd

ORAE (*Otdel'naya Razvedyvatel'naya Aviatsionnaya Eskadrilya* – Independent Reconnaissance Aviation Squadron), also stationed at Bagram. An Su-17M3 'Fitter-K' flown by Capt Mikhail Alexandrov had taken a Stinger hit while returning to Bagram at high altitude, the pilot managing to eject and descending about 29 miles south-west of Kabul.

The 'Frogfoot' pair involved in the C-SAR effort was led by Strepetov, with Maj Alexander Rybakov as his wingman. Initially, they flew at high altitude to avoid the enemy SAMs, but the pilots quickly realised that it would be next to impossible to spot either the ejected pilot or his parachute canopy from such a safe height. Having decided to approach the crash site at low level, they knew that they had to fool the enemy, who were expected to have set up SAM and heavy machine gun ambushes around the downed Su-17M3R, in order to avoid being shot down. The pair started their low-altitude run at about 13 miles from the crash site, the Su-25s entering a neighbouring valley at ultra-low level and high speed, then turning sharply to fly accurately into the mouth of the correct valley.

At this point the pair came under heavy machine gun fire from a position in a village on the right slope, but without effect. However, there were no signs of the crashed Su-17M3R or its pilot in the valley. The Su-25 pilots then realised that they had entered a trap, as they faced a vertical wall at the end of the valley. They immediately made a steep climb away to avoid colliding with the ground, but as their speed was relatively low following the sharp turn to enter the valley, they were barely able to avoid hitting the ridgeline. Popping over the rocky outcrops, Strepetov and Rybakov were at last able to spot, on the slope of a ridge opposite, a parachute canopy and the ejected pilot resting on the ground next to it.

The Su-25 pilots turned back, rolling in to strafe the most probable approaches to the site, then pounded the heavy machine gun emplacement that had fired at them several minutes before in the village at the mouth of the valley. The C-SAR party arrived on the scene 25 minutes after receiving the report that the Su-17M3R pilot had been detected. Thus Capt Mikhail Alexandrov luckily survived a second ejection during his year-long Afghan combat tour, having been recovered 1 hr 40 min after departing his uncontrollable Su-17M3R.

PAKISTAN RAID

One of the lesser-known operations involving Su-25s in Afghanistan was a strike mission recalled by then Capt Alexander Koshkin. In his memoirs, entitled *Shturmovik*, published in Russia in 2012, he revealed a previously undisclosed and clandestine mission flown by four Su-25s to deliver a surprise attack on a huge *Mujahedeen* training camp near the city of Peshawar, well inside Pakistan. This daring strike, in November 1986, was mounted at dawn so that the Su-25 pilots would have sufficient visibility to penetrate Pakistani airspace at ultra-low level and deliver their ordnance using the element of surprise.

To mask the location of its intended target, and thus avoid an early scramble of PAF fighters held on QRA in the area, the four-aircraft Su-25

As a rule the VPU-17A gun pack, containing a twin-barrel GSh-30 cannon, was a last-ditch weapon that was used in the final years of the war in Afghanistan essentially to provide cover for downed aircrew until the arrival of the C-SAR party (*Author's collection*)

A view of an Su-25's R-95Sh engine after the close detonation of a Stinger SAM during an experiment conducted by the Sukhoi Design Bureau at the Faustovo Range near Moscow in early 1987, using 1st Series aircraft c/n 01035. The lessons learned from this experiment were promptly used in the design of a set of additional protective features, implemented on the 10th Series aircraft delivered to 378th OShAP from mid-1987 (*Sukhoi Company*)

formation, led by Capt Koshkin, departed Bagram and maintained a speed of 310 mph in tight formation, thus simulating a single transport aircraft to operators of Pakistani early-warning radar. The formation simulated a landing approach to Jalalabad airfield, not far from the border with Pakistan, and a subsequent go-around. At that moment one of the Su-25s separated from the group, continuing to simulate a transport aircraft that had entered into a holding pattern over the Surubi Dam, while the remaining three jets stayed at low level, invisible to Pakistani early-warning radars, crossed the border and proceeded at 160 ft towards the target. The 'Frogfoots' managed to approach the camp undetected and attacked with complete surprise, making four passes each.

On the first two passes they dropped bombs, on the third they expended rockets and during the fourth the pilots fired their built-in 30 mm cannon. No anti-aircraft fire from the ground was encountered, and the three Su-25s returned to Afghani airspace at ultra-low level well before the PAF fighters could react.

1987-88 ROTATION

The fourth personnel rotation for 378th OShAP included air- and groundcrews drawn from the two squadrons of 187th OShAP, a newly formed attack regiment stationed in Tchernigovka, in the Far East. At the same time the Kandahar-based 3rd AE continued to be staffed by personnel drawn from 80th OShAP, who had commenced their combat deployment in April 1987 and were scheduled for replacement in March 1988.

The new rotation at Bagram received a batch of vastly improved aircraft, the brand-new 10th Series 'Frogfoots' having the full set of survivability-enhancing modifications. They replaced all the surviving 5th, 6th, 7th and 8th Series machines of 1st and 2nd AEs at Bagram. 378th OShAP also operated four Su-25UB two-seaters, but these did not arrive until October 1988, shortly before the end of the rotation. Two of the two-seaters were assigned to 1st AE at Bagram and the other two joined the fleet of 3rd AE, then stationed at Shindand.

On 31 October the senior pilots from the new rotation made their first night training sorties, and on 1 November the newly arrived aircrews of 378th OShAP formally started their independent combat work.

10th Series Su-25 '06', flown by Capt Sergey Emelyushin, was struck by a Stinger on 3 January 1988 during a CAS mission near the city of Khost, sustaining extensive tail-section damage. Nevertheless, Emelyushin managed to return to base and the aircraft was duly repaired (*Andrey Kozhemyakin archive via Author*)

The first loss suffered by the fourth rotation occurred on 26 December 1987 during a pre-planned night mission against a Stinger SAM training camp only seven miles from Bagram. The strike mission was to be performed by two pairs. The first, armed with six ODAB-500P bombs apiece, departed from Bagram and headed towards the target, but soon afterwards one of the aircraft collided with the ground and its ordnance detonated. The pilot, Capt Alexander Plyusin, was killed instantly, and the cause of the accident remains unknown. It seems that the aircraft hit the ground four miles from the airfield due to a late pull-out from a shallow dive attack owing to target fixation experienced by the pilot. The wreckage site was well inside the green zone, in territory firmly held by the local *Mujahedeen* groups at the time, so no C-SAR operation was launched.

A close-up of the badly damaged tail of the Su-25 flown by Capt Sergey Emelyushin on 3 January 1988 (*Andrey Kozhemyakin archive via Author*)

On 3 January 1988 Su-25 '06', flown by Capt Sergey Emelyushin, took a Stinger hit during a CAS sortie in the vicinity of Khost. This was during Operation *Magistral*, a large-scale effort by Soviet forces to clear the road between Kabul and Khost, which had been blocked by opposition forces. The aircraft, hit by the SAM while pulling up after the first dive-attack pass, was badly damaged, its hydraulic system being rendered inoperative. Emelyushin decided to try to fly back to Bagram in his 'Frogfoot', and he duly made an emergency landing with flaps and slats retracted. The brake parachute also failed to deploy because of extensive damage in the tail area and the defunct hydraulics. Consequently, the damaged aircraft failed to stop on the runway and was arrested by the emergency braking net at its end.

On 17 March another Su-25 was reported lost, this time during a training flight to the range near Bagram. Flying as a pair, both jets were armed with S-8 rockets and bombs. En route to the range, the 'Frogfoots' were redirected to provide CAS for a Soviet company in a firefight with the enemy in the nearby green zone. During a firing pass the aircraft flown by 1Lt Andrey Kudryavtsev was badly damaged by fragments from a defective rocket that exploded shortly after launch. Kudryavtsev attempted an emergency landing at Bagram, but this proved impossible due to the jet's poor handling characteristics. He duly ejected at the last possible moment, his powerless Su-25 impacting the ground and exploding inside the airfield perimeter.

Another 'Frogfoot', flown by Capt Vasiliy Turin of 2nd AE, was lost on 27 October 1988 in a landing accident at Bagram. All three undercarriage legs broke off when they hit the edge of the runway threshold at Bagram, leaving the aircraft to skid along on its belly before veering off the tarmac and coming to a halt. The pilot survived the accident unharmed, but his aircraft was so badly damaged that it was subsequently withdrawn from use to serve as a source of spares.

FOURTH PERSONNEL ROTATION VETERAN

In a journal of his experiences, Alexander Araslanov, then a major serving as Deputy CO (Political Affairs) of 1st AE during the fourth rotation period, with 370 combat sorties under his belt, recorded some of the more memorable moments during his combat tour in Afghanistan;

'Bagram is situated approximately in the centre of the wide Charikar Valley that begins at the mouths of the Pandjsher and Salang valleys. The base is at the edge of the green zone, bordering with the desert, where our shooting range is set up. Bagram is heavily guarded by a network of our own and Afghanistan National Army posts, arranged into several rings, with further reinforcement being provided by a motorised rifle division and an airborne troops regiment. Despite all these security measures, bandits penetrate the guarded perimeters from time to time, which means that there is no clear delineation between of own territory and that held by the enemy.

'Each takeoff at Bagram is covered by helicopters hanging in the air and pumping out salvoes of protective flares. Due to the close proximity of the enemy to the airfield, all takeoffs and landings are performed within a narrow, cylindrical-shaped airspace segment through the employment of steep climb-out and glideslope profiles, respectively.

'Having just arrived, and without having experienced combat before, we tackled everything with great enthusiasm and gladly agreed to any mission requests that we received. For example, during the first three days we flew without flares, as the guys we replaced had also flown without them – they initially led us into combat. In the beginning it was a bit scary, but we rapidly got used to the situation. Only two months later did we realise what we had done. It turned out that we had only avoided being shot down because of the enemy's laziness at that time.

'Our first strike mission was conducted against a target in the Pandjsher Cross – a cross-shaped gorge in the first third of the Pandjsher Valley. According to information provided by the Afghani intelligence services, a meeting of Ahmad Shakh Massoud's field commanders had been planned to take place there. This particular pre-planned mission involved a strike package of eight Su-25s, each armed with four S-24 rockets. We reached the target area with ease, but then I got disoriented and spotted the target only after the leader rolled into his dive and all the other pilots in the group had followed him.

'It was a nightmarish situation, unlike anything I had seen before. We rolled in a steep dive, at an angle close to 70 degrees, inside a narrow rocky gorge, at the bottom of which the red roofs of small huts were barely distinguishable. Upon the command "launch", issued by the leader, the space in front of us filled with the smoke trails of unleashed rockets and pumped flares. I had to select my target in a hurry, fire the rockets and pull hard on the control column to initiate climb-out. Passing between rocks, my aircraft was buffeted and proved reluctant to gain altitude. Finally, I saw blue skies again, and the black crosses of the aircraft in the group just in front of me.

'I struggled to understand what was happening around me throughout the mission. I could not work out how the targets had been found in the midst of ridgelines and villages that all looked identical to one another.

'On 21 November 1987 we flew our first strike as part of a composite package. Scheduled for the end of the day, our target was a Stinger missile school. It was located on a steep slope within a narrow gorge not far from Tadjkha village. The strike package comprised Su-17 fighter-bombers and MiG-23 fighters that were also being employed as fighter-bombers.

Our eight-aircraft Su-25 formation had to deliver incendiary bombs [napalm canisters].

'Reaching the target area with our aircraft lit up by the rays of the setting sun, we rolled in to attack from high altitude. The Su-17s, MiG-23s and Su-25s hit the target virtually simultaneously, with the attacking passes made by the three types being separated by the shortest possible intervals. Aircraft rolled in on the target from all directions, performing simultaneous bomb releases and rocket firings. All this action occurred under the soft light of the setting sun, amidst clusters of pumped flares and massed AAA coming up at us from the ground. We were delivering death to the ground, and the ground was shooting death back at us in return. At that moment I realised that Afghanistan was a very special country, as almost 80 per cent of our incendiary bombs failed to initiate fires on the ground. The reason was simple – there was not enough oxygen in the air to fuel fire at such high elevation in the mountains.'

RUTSKOY SHOT DOWN AGAIN

Following a prolonged recovery period after being shot down in April 1986, Alexander Rutskoy returned to Afghanistan in April 1988, having now been promoted to the rank of colonel and appointed Deputy CO (Aviation) of the 40th Army. Despite the seniority of his position, Rutskoy continued flying and fighting the *Mujahedeen* in the same reckless style as he had done in 1986. In fact, his fellow Su-25 pilots claimed that he now seemed to be even more aggressive in his pursuit of the enemy, apparently seeking revenge for his downing. He was also looking forward to receiving more combat awards.

Unsurprisingly, Rutskoy was shot down for a second time on 4 August 1988 while leading 1Lt Andrey Kudryavtsev in an attack on a training camp for air defence personnel that was located some six miles inside Pakistani territory. Rutskoy and his wingman were to mark the target and suppress the air defences for a subsequent strike to be mounted by four more Su-25s. Kudryavtsev was to drop illumination bombs and then the leader was to attack the air defence positions, identified by the muzzle flashes.

As Rutskoy turned towards the target shortly after twilight, his Su-25 ('03') came under attack by a lone PAF F-16A flown by Sqn Ldr Athar Bokhari. The latter had been scrambled from Miranshah air base well in advance of the 'Frogfoots'' arrival. Although the Su-25 pair attempted defensive manoeuvring, spiralling towards the ground after detecting that they had been 'painted' by the F-16's search radar, Rutskoy's aircraft took a hit from an AIM-9L Sidewinder AAM. His wingman was able to escape thanks to his defensive manoeuvres.

Rutskoy managed to eject from the uncontrollable Su-25 and descended safely well inside Pakistani territory. Shortly afterwards he was taken prisoner of war, although he was released two weeks later thanks to diplomatic pressure exerted by both the Soviet government and its intelligence services on their Pakistani counterparts.

Su-25 pilots operating in the Host and Gardez areas, close to the Pakistani border, routinely experienced close encounters with PAF F-16s. As Maj Alexander Araslanov recalled, during a strike mission in mid-October 1988 against pre-planned targets near the border some 13 miles north of the city of Gardez, the aircraft flown by his leader, 1st AE CO Lt Col Anatoly Polyakov, took a powerful hit at high altitude. It was apparently

Col Alexander Rutskoy had a spectacular combat career during his two tours in Afghanistan, being forced to eject twice due to enemy action. On the second occasion, on 4 August 1988, he landed inside Pakistan and was made a prisoner of war by Pakistani authorities – he was released after six weeks in captivity. In the post-Soviet era Rutskoy had a breakneck political career, becoming vice-president of the Russian Federation in 1991 and then launching an unsuccessful coup to remove the President, Boris Yeltsin, in October 1993 (*Author's collection*)

caused by a missile supposedly fired from a Pakistani fighter, as two aerial targets were reportedly detected by Soviet early-warning radar at the time. However, the pilots of the escorting MiG-23MLD fighters had failed to see the attackers on their air-intercept radars. The Su-25 pilots also failed to spot the Pakistani fighter suspected of launching the missile.

Although the detonation inflicted heavy damage on Polyakov's 10th series Su-25, the aircraft remained controllable. The engines worked normally despite the tailcone/brake parachute container having been almost torn out, and the pilot was able to land at Bagram even though his jet was missing half of its starboard tailplane and the port tailplane had been badly damaged. The 'Frogfoot' was duly repaired and returned to service.

HIGH-ALTITUDE BOMBING MISSIONS

The introduction of the Stinger SAM system with longer reach and a jam-resistant seeker caused a sharp increase in the initial attack altitude to 21,450 ft. This later reached 29,700 ft when attacking targets in the mountains, thus giving pilots sufficient height above the terrain to pull up and climb away after delivering their ordnance without having to worry about being hit by SAMs.

For operations in areas with a high Stinger risk the strike packages mainly comprised Su-25s grouped in one or two four-aircraft flights. The diving attack runs saw the aircraft rolling in one after another at 15-second intervals, and only one attack run was made, usually from up-sun, with heading differences of 15 to 20 degrees between individual aircraft. The diving angles in these high-altitude attacks were between 45 and 50 degrees, bomb release and rocket launches being made between 14,800 ft and 16,500 ft above the terrain. The hard-deck limit was set at 11,500 ft. Flares were pumped from the moment of releasing the ordnance until reaching a safe altitude of around 19,800 ft above the terrain. In this way the SAM threat was effectively neutralised, but this degree of safety was achieved at the expense of the effectiveness of the strikes because the high-altitude bomb releases and rocket firings were far from accurate.

And when Su-25 pilots were ordered to perform 70-degree diving attacks the initial altitude from which to start roll-in was increased to 29,700 ft, with bomb release at 21,300 ft to 23,000 ft. The altitude loss after pulling out from the dive ensured that the lowest trajectory point while levelling out remained above 14,760 ft. In the steep dive the Su-25's speed easily reached, and often exceeded, the design limitation of 620 mph.

In his journal recording his experiences in combat, Maj Alexander Araslanov recalled the response of the Su-25 community in-theatre to the vastly increased Stinger threat;

'In December 1987 we began facing a growing hazard. We were quite fatigued, but by then both mission complexity and responsibility had increased greatly. As the enemy

Following the mass introduction of the Stinger SAM in late 1986/early 1987, Su-25 pilots were required to drop bombs from high altitudes, starting climb-out at a minimum altitude of 14,760 ft following bomb release from 24,600 ft down to 21,320 ft (*Andrey Kozhemyakin archive via Author*)

began setting up ambushes high in the mountains the Stingers' reach increased to 21,300 ft. That is why we were ordered to fly to and from the target areas at a cruising altitude of up to 26,200 ft.

'Furthermore, in addition to the difficulties associated with target detection from such heights, we faced another serious issue. Our attack aircraft was tailor-made to survive on the battlefield, being well protected against fragments and stray projectiles, including those of larger calibre, but it proved ill suited to high-altitude operations. Of course it could fly at these heights without any problem, but its un-pressurised cockpit forced us to wear oxygen masks all the time and breathe pure oxygen. Initially it seemed our health was unaffected by these high-altitude operations, but later on I realised that it was painful to breathe air on the ground just after landing. The pain was felt in the spine, just behind the chest. Our doctors refused to pay any attention to such minor health issues, and when asked to explain the cause of the pain they described it as an oxygen-induced burn-out of the lungs. In fact this specific pain was caused by the decompression effect experienced during steep dives. Under such conditions atmospheric pressure changes rapidly, causing partial separation of the lung pleura.

'We also faced another, much greater, in-flight danger – disruption of the oxygen supply when the aircraft's oxygen equipment failed. Fortunately, this was a rare occurrence. In addition, pilots sometimes simply forgot to connect their oxygen masks to the oxygen supply line, and suffered hypoxia as a result at high altitude. At least two pilots from the regiment we had replaced perished in such circumstances, both of them losing consciousness while performing a high-altitude night flight. Our aircraft lacked an autopilot, so when the pilot failed to grip the control column the Su-25 tended to roll and gradually lose altitude.'

COVERING THE SOVIET WITHDRAWAL

The plan for the withdrawal of Soviet troops from Afghanistan, numbering about 106,000, was approved by the Minister of Defence, Marshall Dmitry Yazov, on 7 April 1988. It called for two pull-out phases, the first running from 15 May to 15 August 1988 and the second between 1 September 1988 and 14 February 1989.

378th OShAP was given an important role in the withdrawal plan, and it was among the last Soviet units scheduled to leave Afghanistan. The regiment was tasked with making non-stop attacks against possible enemy positions and bases alongside the Soviet forces' withdrawal routes, and with illuminating the perimeter around the retreating columns during the night to counter and prevent ambushes, attacks and shelling under the cover of darkness.

In line with the withdrawal plan, 378th OShAP despatched an eight-strong detachment to Kabul airport to provide this facility with protection from rocket attacks and to give air support to withdrawing Soviet garrisons from Gardez, Asadabad and Jalalabad. The detachment arrived at Kabul on 3 May 1988 and immediately set about its work, countering the increased threat of rocket attacks against the airfield from nearby mountains by maintaining permanent patrols above possible launch areas. Upon detecting fired rockets by the dust cloud at their launch site, the Su-25s were cleared to attack immediately.

CHAPTER FOUR

The devastating fire at Kabul airport on 24 June 1988 consumed nine Su-25s that were lined up close to each other and ready to go, fully fuelled and loaded with weapons. The conflagration was started by a direct rocket hit on one of the 'Frogfoots' (*Andrey Kozhemyakin archive via Author*)

The worst 'Frogfoot' losses sustained by the VVS during the war in Afghanistan occurred on the night of 24 June when nine out of ten aircraft at Kabul were destroyed on the flightline. A direct rocket hit set one of the fully fuelled and armed Su-25s ablaze, and the ferocious fire quickly consumed eight more aircraft that were parked very close to each other. Only one Su-25 survived after groundcrew managed to get it running and taxied it away to safety. Four days previously, on 20 June, another 'Frogfoot' had been reported destroyed on the tarmac at Kandahar, again by a direct rocket or mine hit.

At the beginning of July 1988 378th OShAP received five 10th Series Su-25s, previously operated by 372nd OIShAE (*Otdel'naya Instruktorskaya Shturmovaya Aviatsionnaya Eskadrilya* – Independent Instructor Ground-Attack Aviation Squadron) within 1038th Combat Training and Aircrew Conversion Centre at Djizak, in Uzbekistan. These aircraft were delivered to the Kabul-based detachment as urgent attrition replacements following the painful loss of nine jets on 24 June.

3rd AE left Kandahar in July 1988 and initially deployed to Shindand for two weeks, before relocating to the unit's new permanent base at Bagram. From here its Su-25s continued to provide top cover at Kandahar airfield, protecting transport aircraft and helicopters from SAM launches when taking off and landing and attacking hostile rocket- and mortar-firing positions around the airfield. On 7 August six 3rd AE Su-25s deployed to Kunduz airfield, while the rest were ferried to Bagram. The unit remained at the latter base until October, when it returned to Shindand once again.

In his journal 1st AE pilot Alexander Araslanov recalled the general situation in Afghanistan in October 1988, by which point the Soviet withdrawal was in full swing;

'The situation in-country had turned into a complete mess! Asmar had been overrun by the armed opposition and Asadabad and Jalalabad were completely cut off and ready for capitulation. Local troops had been unable to hold and protect all of the cities and points abandoned by our forces. Three alternatives were conceived for our withdrawal, the first of which was the scheduled one, currently in progress. The second called for a massed push through the Salang Pass in one stream, and the third, should the Salang Pass be blocked, was to leave behind all the equipment and evacuate the troops by air – this would be a last resort.'

During the fourth personnel rotation period of 378th OShAP, between 28 October 1987 and 17 November 1988, 11,779 combat sorties were flown totalling 8809 flying hours. Of these, 138 sorties (1.2 per cent of the total) were dedicated to CAS missions, 7276 (62 per cent) to pre-planned strikes, 1522 (13 per cent) to free hunting and patrolling and 1410 (12 per cent) to aerial mine-laying. As many as 2756 rockets were fired and 42,157 bombs dropped, plus a further 12,691 miscellaneous bombs (mainly illumination and smoke type).

LAST PERSONNEL ROTATION

206th OShAP, home-based at Kobrin, in Belarus, was the last VVS unit to deploy its air- and groundcrews to Afghanistan, personnel undertaking the fifth, and last, rotation period of 378th OShAP between October 1988 and February 1989. This operation also involved a number of air- and groundcrews from 90th OShAP, home-based at Artsiz. Together with their colleagues from 206th OShAP, they were assigned to 1st and 2nd AEs at Bagram. 3rd AE, operating at that time from Shindand, was staffed by air- and groundcrews provided by 368th OShAP, home-based at Pruzhani, in Belarus, who started their Afghan combat tour in May 1988 and soldiered on until February 1989.

On 22 October 1988 personnel were ferried to Bagram by Ilyushin Il-76 airlifters, and after a short in-theatre familiarisation programme the last rotation with 378th OShAP began its independent combat work on 29 October. In addition to the main base at Bagram, eight Su-25s continued to be forward deployed at Kabul, their primary mission being to patrol over the airport and prevent rocket and mortar attacks. These were proving to be a serious problem, and the first sorties targeting rocket-launch positions around the capital city were flown on 13 November 1988. Pilots reported the destruction of four launchers in the form of primitive tripods and some 20 122 mm rockets, as well as the killing of 15 insurgents. During the night of 13 November, however, a *Mujahedeen* rocket attack scored a direct hit on an airport building, killing eight Su-25 pilots from Kobrin.

Missions undertaken by 378th OShAP's last rotation mainly consisted of strikes against pre-planned targets, with CAS and free-hunting sorties having been drastically scaled back. Targeting information was delivered to the regiment's planning cell the day before the mission was to be flown, with typical targets including *Mujahedeen* troop concentrations, weapons/ammunition storage depots and fortified defensive positions. Fuel/air explosive and HE bombs were the main weapons used in pre-planned missions, together with 122 mm, 240 mm and 250 mm rockets. In fact, the vast majority of the pre-planned strikes were designated as 'scorched earth' area-saturation missions, and

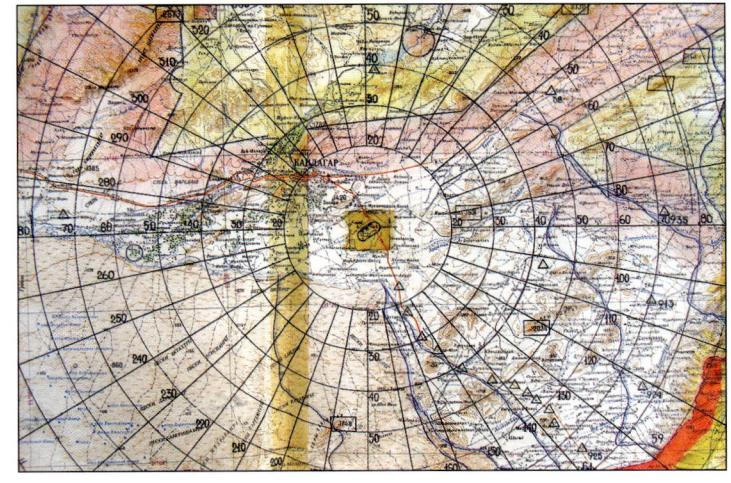

A pilot's map of the Kandahar area in 1988, with the airfield marked in the centre. The free-hunting areas for Mi-24 and Su-25 operations, conducted mostly at night, were primarily located south of the city towards the border with Pakistan (*Author's collection*)

All of the Su-25 missions flown in Afghanistan involved a single pair or group of pairs. Flying over inhospitable terrain was mentally challenging, and it was very difficult to organise effective C-SAR operations to recover ejected pilots in the high-rising, snow-covered mountains. The highest altitude from which an ejected 'Frogfoot' pilot was recovered by an Mi-8MT helicopter was 11,800 ft above sea level, on 3 December 1986 (*Andrey Kozhemyakin archive via Author*)

these had little or no effect on enemy operations.

The night combat sorties of the last rotation were flown by the most experienced pilots only due to their very high workload. 378th OShAP would typically undertake three combat missions in the morning, followed by mission planning in the late afternoon and two or three more sorties at the night. This busy schedule was maintained for weeks on end.

The Su-25s were also involved in Operation *Typhoon* in early January 1989, spending three days attacking a large number of pre-planned targets along the main road in the Pandjsher Valley and the Salang Pass that was being used for the withdrawal of the last Soviet columns towards the border checkpoints.

378th OShAP's final pilot loss occurred on 7 January 1989 during a free-hunting daytime mission conducted by a pair of Su-25s from Kabul. The aircraft flown by the wingman, 1Lt Boris Gordienko, inexplicably entered a steep dive from 22,700 ft and hit the ground near the village of Maidenshahr 17 miles west of Kabul. The wreckage was located in an inaccessible high-altitude mountainous area some 13,000 ft above sea level and next to a ridgeline, so no C-SAR operation was launched to recover the pilot's remains. The most likely cause of the accident was the failure of Gordienko's oxygen supply system in high-altitude flight, causing the pilot to lose consciousness due to hypoxia and leaving him unable to recover from the dive.

The Bagram-based main force of 378th OShAP began to withdraw from Afghanistan on 31 January 1989, flying to Kokayty, in the Soviet republic of Uzbekistan, and then on to Kizil-Arvat. The latter site was used as a temporary staging base for the Su-25 fleet to gather at before the ferry flight to the final destination at Pruzhani. Shindand-based 3rd AE returned to the Soviet Union on 1 February, flying to Kizil-Arvat following a refuelling stop at Mary. The Su-25 detachment operating from Mazar-e-Sharif completed its combat work and flew to Kizil-Arvat via Mary on 10 February.

The fifth, and last, rotation of 378th OShAP completed 6628 combat sorties between 29 October 1988 and 10 February 1989, 812 of which were flown at night. The total combat flying time was 7300 hrs.

By the time it pulled out of Afghanistan after almost ten years of fighting, the Soviet Union had lost 14,453 servicemen killed in action, as well as 333 helicopters and 118 fixed-wing aircraft. A significant number of aircraft were damaged beyond economical repair in combat and subsequently withdrawn from use. A great many more were written off for non-combat-related reasons, although these aircraft were not included in the official war loss statistics. The official figures for Su-25 combat losses in Afghanistan were 12 pilots killed in action and 23 aircraft destroyed, although the total number of 'Frogfoots' written off (either in combat or operationally) in the air and on the ground was no fewer than 38. The total number of combat sorties flown by the Su-25 force during the war was around 60,000.

ACTION AFTER SOVIET BREAK UP

Just before the dissolution of the Soviet Union on 26 December 1991, the VVS frontal aviation branch had on strength as many as eight Su-25-equipped independent attack regiments, directly subordinated to the aviation command authorities of their respective military districts or regional air armies. Each of these regiments had three component squadrons and a command flight, with a fleet, as a rule, of 40 single-seaters and four to six two-seaters. Additionally, the Su-25 was operated by no fewer than five dedicated test and evaluation, air display and conversion-to-type training squadrons, as well as by one instructor attack regiment. The Soviet naval aviation service also had three independent attack regiments and a dedicated aircrew training and research squadron on strength in the late 1980s.

In the early post-Soviet era the Russian Air Force (RuAF), faced with growing unrest around the fringes of the former USSR, rapidly switched from a Cold War posture to one of internal policing. In this new setting the ubiquitous jet attack aircraft saw faithful service in numerous local conflicts that erupted in what is now known as the Commonwealth of Independent States (CIS, the Soviet Union's successor). The first of these was the inter-ethnical war between North Ossetia and Ingushetia in 1992, the second involved Abkhazia and Georgia in 1992-94 and the third was the war between Azerbaijan and Armenia over the territory of Nagorni Karabakh in 1992-94. The fourth local conflict in the early/mid-1990s was the Russian campaign mounted against the Islamic fundamentalists in Tajikistan in 1992-94, followed by the campaigns of the Russian military in Chechnya in 1994-96 and 1999-2002. Finally, Russia fought a five-day war with Georgia over the territory of South Ossetia in 2008.

No fewer than 570 'Frogfoots' of all versions were in active service with the VVS and the AV-MF (*Aviatsiya Voenno-Morskogo Flota* – Naval Aviation service) in 1991, including up to 96 two-seaters, and a small number of early-production Su-25s were held in long-term storage. This Su-25 of 960th ShAP, home-based at Primorsko-Akhtarsk, was used in anger in both Chechen campaigns, flying most of its missions while forward-deployed at Mozdok. It is seen here armed with S-24 240 mm rockets (*Dmitry Pichugin via Author*)

This Armenian Su-25UBK was one of a pair of two-seaters and six Su-25Ks secretively delivered by Russian military authorities to their Armenian counterparts in December 1992, the aircraft being taken from 802nd UAP (*Author's collection*)

FIGHTING IN THE NORTH CAUCASUS

Alexander Koshkin, a seasoned Afghan war veteran and at the time CO of the Su-25-equipped 3rd AE of 802nd UAP (*Uchebno-Trenirovochnyy Aviatsionnyy Polk –* Basic Training Aviation Regiment), within the structure of the Krasnodar Higher Pilot Training School, recalled that in October 1992 his squadron was given an urgent order to deploy to Mozdok airfield, in the Russian republic of North Ossetia. The main purpose of this deployment to Russia's troubled North Caucasus region was a show of force to both warring parties – the small but warlike and temperamental Ossetian and Ingushetian nations populating the newly formed Russian republics of North Ossetia and Ingushetia. These nations were then engaged in a bloody inter-ethnical conflict that had erupted owing to a dispute over the exact location of the borderline.

In addition to the show-of-force missions, flying low and fast over concentrations of militants in both republics, the RuAF Su-25s deployed to Mozdok performed visual reconnaissance sorties aimed at monitoring the movement of illegal armed formations of both ethnicities by reporting the current position of their vehicle columns. Most missions flown in the combat zone took place in daylight, and no opposition was encountered. During show-of-force missions at night Su-25s from 802nd UAP expended illumination bombs over areas where Ossetian and Ingushetian militants had engaged each other with small arms and heavy machine gun fire. The effectiveness of nocturnal show-of-force fly-bys was further amplified by the modest height at which they were performed.

ARMENIA AND AZERBAIJAN

In this bloody and protracted inter-ethnical conflict between two former Soviet republics, both warring sides used the Su-25 in anger. All combat operations took place in the breakaway Nagorni Karabakh enclave, with the predominant Armenian population fighting to gain independence from Azerbaijan and join mainland Armenia.

Azerbaijan received its first Su-25 when it was hijacked from 80th OShAP in Sital-Chai on 8 April 1992 by Azeri pilot Lt Vaghit Kurbanov, who was assisted by two technicians of Azeri nationality. This aircraft was used from 8 May to conduct bombing missions against the Armenian military forces stationed in the capital, Stepanakert, as well as in border zones within Armenian territory. Based at Evlakh airfield, in Azerbaijan, not far from the fighting, the lone 10th Series 'Frogfoot' continued to fly combat missions for two months, mainly attacking cities and villages but failing to inflict any significant losses on Armenian forces. For instance, during its first two days of combat operations its bomb attacks killed 30 civilians and wounded 120 in the city of Stepanakert.

On 9 May the Su-25, flown by Kurbanov, fired at an Armenian Yak-40 passenger aircraft ferrying refugees and wounded from Stepanakert to Armenia, inflicting some damage. The burning Yak-40 made an undercarriage-up emergency landing on flat terrain and was completely consumed by the post-landing fire, although all the passengers survived. Kurbanov also attacked a Russian Mi-8 transport helicopter flying in Armenian airspace, but without success. The hijacked Su-25 that terrorised the Nagorni Karabakh enclave was at last shot down by Armenian forces on 13 June 1992, killing the pilot. The remains of the aircraft, including a fin adorned with Azerbaijani Air Force insignia, were shown on Armenian television.

Azerbaijan continued operating the type, having purchased five additional Su-25s. Their source has not been revealed, but these machines probably came from countries such as Georgia, Ukraine or Turkmenistan. They were rushed into combat for the first time in August 1992, flown by mercenary pilots from other ex-Soviet republics. Used mainly to attack Stepanakert, the Su-25s dropped cluster and large-calibre HE bombs that inflicted heavy casualties among the civilians in Armenian cities and villages. No fewer than 180 cluster bombs and 100 heavy-calibre HE bombs are reported to have been dropped between November 1992 and May 1994, as well as eight FAE bombs. The Armenian armed forces eventually claimed to have downed four of the newly delivered 'Frogfoots' following the strengthening of air defences in Nagorni Karabakh between October 1992 and April 1994. The first was downed on 10 October 1993, the second on 15 January 1994, the third on 12 April and the fourth 11 days later.

Armenia also introduced the type in 1992-93, taking delivery of eight Su-25s, including two two-seaters, in the form of military aid clandestinely provided by Russia. The donated aircraft were secretly ferried to Armenia from Krasnodar and Mozdok in four batches. The first two ferry flights were led by Maj Alexander Koshkin, CO of 3rd AE of 802nd UAP at Krasnodar, who recalled that both sorties, made in December 1992, were conducted in tight formation with an An-12 transport. This was done intentionally so that the formation would appear as a single target on civilian and military air traffic control and early-warning radars as it passed over foreign countries. This particular An-12 had previously transported humanitarian supplies from Russia to Lenianakan (now Gumri) airfield in Armenia, having the correct authorisation for such international flights.

Two pairs of 'Frogfoots' were ferried from Mozdok in consecutive weeks and, as Koshkin recalled, the most difficult element of the mission was the formation landing approach and touchdown with the An-12. The Su-25 pilots had to be as close to the transport aircraft as possible so as to avoid their detection in the final stages of the flight. In early 1993 four more ex-RuAF Su-25s were clandestinely handed over to the newly formed Armenian Air Force. In November of that year a brand new 'Frogfoot' of the Georgian Air Force (GeAF) was hijacked by a Russian mercenary pilot in Georgia and flown to Armenia.

The newly delivered Armenian Su-25s saw their fair share of use in anger until the end of hostilities in May 1994, bombing targets inside Azerbaijan and on the frontline in the Nagorni Karabakh area. One aircraft was reported lost in action on 18 January 1994, supposedly gunned down by friendly fire. This bloody war, which lasted until 12 May 1994, was eventually won by Armenia. The Nagorni Karabakh enclave was cleared of Azerbaijani troops and subsequently connected with the mainland.

80th OShAP, based at Sital-Chai near the Azerbaijan capital, Baku, had managed to stay intact (excluding the aforementioned Su-25 hijacked on 8 April 1992 by Kurbanov) within the RuAF after the break-up of the Soviet Union and the onset of the war between Azerbaijan and Armenia over the Nagorni Karabakh. The regiment was subsequently withdrawn to Russia shortly after the commencement of hostilities in the region. While the unit was still stationed at Sital-Chai the Azerbaijani authorities had applied strong pressure on 80th OShAP's CO, Col Alexander Golovanov, to hand over his aircraft and the regiment's support equipment and ammunition. He had flatly refused, however.

Shortly thereafter 80th OShAP received the long-awaited withdrawal order from the Commander-in-Chief of the Trans-Caucasian Military District, calling for the regiment's aircraft and personnel to be ferried to Buturlinovka airfield in the European part of Russia. The mass departure from Sital-Chai took place on 10 June 1992. All personnel and the regiment's support equipment were promptly loaded onto Il-76 transports, which then led the Su-25s back to Russia. Having taken the regimental flag with him in the cockpit of his 'Frogfoot', Col Golovanov was the last Russian officer to leave the base. After taking off in a two-seat Su-25UB, 80th OShAP's CO turned back, rolled in and unleashed all of the 80 mm rockets in the aircraft's B8M1 packs at the buildings and runway of the abandoned airfield.

GEORGIA AND ABKHAZIA

The war between Georgia and its breakaway province of Abkhazia erupted shortly after the Georgian government decided to intervene with military force in the autonomous province, which was populated by ethnic Abkhazians. The formal reason given by Georgia for the intervention was to ensure the security of the strategic railway linking Russia and the war-torn former Soviet republic of Armenia.

On 14 August 1992, at the height of the holiday season, Georgian National Guard units invaded Abkhazia, claiming that their main objective was to provide protection for the railway, while the Abkhazian authorities stated that this act was the occupation of an autonomous province. The Georgian troops that performed the initial invasion numbered some 2000, and they were equipped with 58 armoured vehicles and a significant number of artillery pieces and multiple rocket launchers. The Abkhazian provincial government quickly organised territorial defence with irregular military forces, although they proved ineffective in stopping the Georgian advance. As a result Georgian forces quickly occupied the province's capital, the Black Sea coastal city of Sukhumi, and then in late August seized Gagra, another important city in the autonomous province.

Georgian troops eventually halted their offensive in Abkhazia following an ill-fated attack on the city of Nizhniye Eshery on 31 August, and the consequent order issued by the president, Eduard Shevarnadze, to discontinue the invasion. After that the frontline was stabilised on both sides of the Gumista River.

In October the Abkhazian forces, bolstered by numerous volunteers from the North Caucasus republics and Russia, and using weapons captured from the Georgians, taken from Russian forces at Gudauta

An Su-25UB of 802nd UAP, home-based at Krasnodar and armed with R-60 AAMs, flies over the Black Sea in the vicinity of Gudauta airfield during the unit's secretive combat deployment to Abkhazia between March and November 1993. This machine displays a large Russian flag on the fin and white wingtip pods, both markings having been hastily applied during the deployment to enable rapid identification by friendly forces on the ground (*Andrey Kozhemyakin archive via Author*)

or handed over by the Russians on other occasions, launched a swift counteroffensive and regained control of Gagra. Thus, by late 1992, the warring parties had established a classical frontline some 7.5 miles long, which remained stable until the second half of 1993.

Some eight Su-25s, operated by the newly established GeAF, saw combat during the war. These brand-new 'Frogfoots', powered by uprated R-195 engines, were taken from undelivered stocks at the Tbilisi aviation plant. In mid/late 1992 between eight and fifteen Su-25s were reported to be in various states of assembly at the plant, and most of them were completed and delivered to the GeAF. Flown by pilots of Georgian nationality who had previously served with the VVS, they were rushed into combat soon after the offensive commenced in Abkhazia.

GeAF 'Frogfoots' were reportedly used in anger for the first time on 28 September 1992 when they bombed the Abkhazian rear areas. Later on they were routinely used to bomb Abkhazian forces defending the city of Gudauta, as well as the frontline on the banks of the Gumista River, from where Abkhazian field artillery shelled the city of Sukhumi. As many as six GeAF Su-25s were lost in combat, one of them supposedly to friendly fire, up to the cessation of hostilities in September 1993. The first GeAF loss occurred on 11 October 1992 near Eshera when an Su-25 was hit by a 9K38 Igla (SA-18 'Grouse') SAM fired by Abkhazian irregulars. Its pilot, Slava Djabua, bailed out, descended by parachute into the sea and then disappeared without trace. The second Su-25 was brought down near the village of Merkula, on the frontline, on 6 February 1993. Its pilot, Tamaz Nadirashvili, successfully ejected and was captured by the Abkhazians in Mokva village. On 1 May another GeAF Su-25 was downed by a Russian 9K33 Osa-AKM (SA-8 'Gecko') self-propelled missile system near the cities of Nizhniye Eshery and Gudauta.

It is noteworthy that after several GeAF Su-25 attacks against targets in and around Gudauta (the last of which was mounted on 26 April) that caused numerous military and civilian causalities, the Russian Army promptly deployed 9K33 Osa-AKM and 9K37 Buk mobile SAM systems to Abkhazia. RuAF pilot Mikhail Pavlov, who was serving with 802nd

Photographed during their secretive combat deployment to Gudauta, in Abkhazia, in 1993, pilots Capt Mikhail Pavlov (right) and Capt Alexander Yakovlev of 802nd UAP and later 461st ShAP stand in front of Su-25K '28', armed with S-24 rockets (*Andrey Kozhemyakin archive via Author*)

Su-25K '34' of 461st ShAP is lined up at the end of the runway at Gudauta, in Abkhazia, ready to lead a second 'Frogfoot' aloft on another combat mission. The aircraft is armed with four B8M rocket pods and two R-60 AAMs for self defence, the latter carried in case of an encounter with Georgian Su-25s in the combat zone (*Andrey Kozhemyakin archive via Author*)

The large and accurate S-25 tube-launched rocket, two of which are seen here being fired by an Su-25BM of 899th ShAP, was one of the most powerful weapons used by the Su-25 in Afghanistan and all the ensuing local conflicts. It has proven well suited to dealing with small-size hardened targets thanks to the rocket's accuracy and powerful warhead (*Vasiliy Fedosenko via Author*)

UAP's detachment at Gudauta at the time, recalled;

'On 1 May 1993 in Abkhazia I saw with my own eyes how our SAM units managed to shoot down the leader of a Su-25 pair, while the wingman remained untouched, avoiding three missiles directed at him by sharp manoeuvring, descending in a steep spiral down to ultra-low level.'

The Su-25 pair engaged by the 9K33 Osa-AKM SAMs had approached the target area in level flight at an altitude of 14,800 ft and a speed of 373 mph. The Osa-AKM systems launched their missiles against the pair at a slant range of about 16,400 ft (5,000m). The pilot of the downed 'Frogfoot', Capt Rezo Naurashvili, managed to eject into captivity, and remained a prisoner of war until 1996.

On 4 July a fourth GeAF Su-25 was reported lost near Sukhumi. Its pilot, Kakha Tvauri, ejected into the sea and was then rescued by Georgian forces. A fifth loss followed just nine days later, and the sixth, and last, 'Frogfoot' to be destroyed was hit over the village of Tavisupleba, near Sukhumi, on 24 September. Its pilot, GeAF Deputy C-in-C Col Izani Tservadze, had no choice but to eject, and he was subsequently killed after descending by parachute into enemy-held territory.

Following the loss of Naurashvili the GeAF stopped conducting attack missions around Gudauta, its Su-25s remaining active only over the frontline and around the city of Sukhumi, besieged by the Abkhazians. As many as 215 combat missions are reported to have been flown by GeAF Su-25s during the conflict in Abkhazia in 1992-93.

RUAF OPERATIONS IN ABKHAZIA

The RuAF deployed its 'Frogfoot' force for the first time in Abkhazia on 1 September 1992. A detachment of four Su-25s and two Su-25UBs drawn from 186th IShAP (*Instruktorskiy Shturmovoy Aviatsionnyy Polk* – Instructor Ground-Attack Aviation Regiment) of the Borisoglebsk Higher Pilot School, home-based in Buturlinovka, was stationed at the former Soviet Air Defence forces airfield at Gudauta, near the Black Sea coast. It continued operations until 28 April 1993, completing 231 combat sorties, 170 of which were dedicated to attacking ground targets. The remaining 61 were aerial reconnaissance flights.

Krasnodar-based 802nd UAP also despatched a detachment of nine Su-25s and one Su-25UB two-seater to Gudauta. The group arrived at the forward operating location on 2 March 1993, initially complementing and later replacing the aircrews and aircraft from Buturlinovka, which were despatched on another combat tour shortly thereafter, this time in the troubled former Soviet republic of Tajikistan.

The RuAF Su-25s were clandestinely deployed into Abkhazia, the Russian government never openly acknowledging the fact that it had stationed military forces in-theatre to support the local separatists in their war against the Georgian invasion, thus maintaining the power balance in the region. During their deployment to Gudauta the

'Frogfoot' pilots had to fly combat missions without carrying any identity documents, and the combat sorties flown were formally accounted for as training flights.

802nd UAP's detachment was also reinforced by two pilots from the Lipetsk-based Combat Training and Aircrew Conversion Centre, who arrived at Gudauta in mid-March. They were tasked with flying a range of even more secretive combat missions, by both day and night, using 802nd UAP aircraft – the pilots from Lipetsk never shared any mission details with their colleagues from Krasnodar. In June 1993 3rd AE of 802nd UAP was used as the basis for establishing 461st ShAP, an all-new two-squadron combat unit stationed at Krasnodar-Central airfield.

802nd UAP Su-25s operating in Abkhazia received Vympel R-60 (AA-8 'Aphid') air-to-air heat-seeking missiles in 1993 following three encounters with GeAF Su-25s. Two of these involved pilots from 186th IShAP and the third a pilot from 802nd UAP. As Mikhail Pavlov recalled, an 802nd UAP 'Frogfoot' flown by Lt Col Nikolay Inkov engaged a GeAF Su-25 during a training sortie, the RuAF jet being armed only with its 30 mm built-in cannon. However, it transpired that both pilots were sufficiently experienced to be able to deny their opponent an attacking opportunity. To make RuAF Su-25s visually distinguishable from their GeAF counterparts their wingtip airbrake pods were painted white and their fins had large tricolour Russian flags painted on both sides.

In the spring and summer months of 1993 the RuAF Su-25s continued operating clandestinely, with Russia denying any involvement of its forces in support of the Abkhazians. In reality the 'Frogfoots' had mounted numerous attacks against the Georgian forces around the coastal city of Sukhumi and over the frontline along the Gumista River. In addition, APCs and trucks on the move in the rear areas, transporting men and supplies to the frontal zone, had been repeatedly targeted. Alexander Koshkin, CO of 3rd AE within 802nd UAP at the time of the deployment and then CO of 1st AE of newly established 461st ShAP, who amassed a total of 820 combat sorties in Afghanistan, North Ossetia, Abkhazia, Tajikistan and the first Chechen campaign, recalled some of the more memorable moments during the combat missions he flew in Abkhazia;

'In 1993 I logged 50 to 60 combat sorties in Abkhazia, attacking various Georgian military targets. I'm very proud of the fact that all the young pilots I had instructed before going to this deployment survived, and nobody was lost in combat.

'I believe that it is a must when in action to always remember that your enemy has eyes and ears, making him well capable of seeing and listening. Therefore, if it is impossible to render him blind and deaf, you should invent a deception that masks your approach to the target. I did exactly this in an effective combat mission that I led during the Abkhazian deployment. We received intelligence information that a Georgian military column with tanks, armoured vehicles and trucks bringing reinforcements to the frontline was on the move near the coastal city of Poti. To approach the target area unseen, and thus allow us to make maximum use of the element of surprise, I decided to apply a trick – perhaps not a very ethical one, but it worked pretty well, and in the event the mission objective was achieved.

'We took off from Gudauta in a four-aircraft formation and initially turned to the right, as if we were heading towards the Russian city of Adler. Just before reaching Adler, however, we lined up in a tight formation, turned and started climbing to 27,900 ft, entering into the busy international air route that ran out over the sea towards the Turkish city of Trabzon, simulating that we were an airliner. When abeam of Poti we rolled in a steep descent down to ultra-low level and turned east. Flying at between 500 ft and 660 ft, we were in the target area within three to four minutes and immediately spotted the vehicle column that was to be attacked. There were no main battle tanks, however – the convoy consisted of armoured vehicles and trucks only. As a result of the surprise strike two APCs and seven to nine trucks were set ablaze in two attacking passes. We then returned to Gudauta at ultra-low level, without once being shot at by the enemy air defences.

'Another mission called for us to mount a strike against a Georgian corps-level HQ in the village of Kolasuri, near Sukhumi. We had intelligence information stating that there was a concentration of men and military vehicles and a fuel dump in this area. The Georgian forces, however, had very strong air defences there, consisting of ZSU-23-4 Shilka AAA [a self-propelled system with four radar-directed 23 mm cannon] and medium-range SAM systems, so the risk of being shot down was pretty high.

'I asked the squadron navigation officer to calculate the probability of hitting the target using toss-bombing, and he had to plot the initial point for starting the attack run. The bomb had to be tossed on a 45-degree climb-out while pulling 5g, releasing it three seconds after initiating the manoeuvre. The distance from the non-directional beacon [NDB] at Gudauta to the ordnance release point would be covered in three to four minutes at ultra-low altitude. I knew the enemy would detect us, but with a serious delay, allowing us to get close enough to execute the bomb-toss manoeuvre and escape just in time. In this way the probability of being hit by the Shilka AAA systems would be negligible.

'We took off at dawn, still in twilight, maintaining a tight formation and keeping 50 ft apart, with 7 ft to 10 ft vertical separation. Immediately after takeoff we turned right towards Russia, but before reaching Adler we descended to ultra-low level and turned back, heading for Gudauta. We flew over land directly into the airfield's NDB, passing overhead at 80 ft to 100 ft altitude, and upon crossing the coastline descended further down to 50 ft, heading directly for Sukhumi. Just after sighting the city's lighthouse I initiated the tossing attack manoeuvre. All four Su-25s, each armed with six 500 kg bombs, entered a climb and released their ordnance upon my command. We then continued the looping manoeuvre and rolled off the top to head back home, again descending to ultra-low level. In my rear-view mirror I noticed the hosing fire of tracers from the ZSU-23-4 systems, but it had no effect.

'The next day we received the bomb damage assessment report on that particular mission, informing us that some 200 enemy combatants had been killed when the building housing the corps HQ was destroyed. A number of fuel storage tanks had also been blown up.'

The only Russian Su-25 loss in Abkhazia was reported in September 1993, and it occurred under non-combat conditions. The aircraft flown by

Lt Col Chaplitskiy, head of the flight safety section of 1st GShAD (*Guards Shturmovaya Aviatsionnaya Diviziya* – Guards Ground-Attack Aviation Division) at Krasnodar, hit the sea not far from Gudauta during a mission to simulate an air target at ultra-low altitude, killing the pilot. Chaplitskiy's mission was intended to train the crews of the SAM systems defending Gudauta, and at the same time check the range at which the Russian air defence radars would detect aerial targets approaching at ultra-low level from the sea. During a high-banked turn just above a glassy sea the pilot clipped the water's surface with the wingtip of his Su-25 and crashed.

On 28 September 1993 Abkhazian forces managed to seize the provincial capital city of Sukhumi, and shortly thereafter cleared the entire province of Georgian forces, thus allowing Abkhazia to proclaim its independence. Consequently, the RuAF Su-25 detachment returned to Krasnodar in November that year.

MUSLIM INSURGENCY IN TAJIKISTAN

RuAF Su-25s were also rushed into combat against radical Muslim opposition groups in Tajikistan that had received significant support in the form of reinforcements, weapons and manpower from their ideological brothers in neighbouring Afghanistan. These groups launched a massed offensive against the government in Dushanbe in mid-1993, and it was only because of the decisive and prompt involvement of Russian forces that the local government was saved from being ousted. Russian troops (both border guards and the 201st Mechanised Infantry Division) were also responsible for border security, personnel trying to seal off the previously porous 862-mile border with Afghanistan that ran along the Pyandj River and through rugged mountainous terrain.

A squadron of 'Frogfoots' belonging to 186th IShAP was urgently ordered to deploy to Kokayty airfield in neighbouring Uzbekistan, 19 miles from the border with Tajikistan. This war deployment was in response to the assassination of 25 Russian border guard soldiers by Tajikistani Islamist rebels at the 12th Border Post. The squadron, equipped with ten Su-25BM/UBs, arrived in-theatre on 24 July 1993 and immediately commenced flying bombing sorties. Just 24 hours after the deployment had commenced, a four-aircraft group launched two attacks against a hardened defensive position near the village of Vari, completely destroying it. Three days later an improvised bridge across the Piandj River was struck by Su-25s just as a large group of rebels were infiltrating into Tajikistan. Some 150 Islamist fighters were reportedly killed during this mission, with three improvised bridge lanes and ten boats being destroyed in three individual strikes conducted by four-aircraft formations.

On 23 October 1993 a group of four Su-25s again attacked a rebel base in the foothills of the Pamir mountains, and on 28 November a concentration of enemy fighters came under attack from the air.

During the first RuAF 'Frogfoot' deployment period as many as 859 combat sorties were logged – 236 of these were pre-planned strikes against ground targets or for aerial mine-laying and 423 were dedicated to visual aerial reconnaissance. Some 1500 Islamist combatants were reported killed and four rebel bases destroyed, as were 18 improvised bridges across the Pyandj River and 12 hardened defensive positions. During the early months of the deployment, which proved to be the most intensive period of operations, the Su-25s delivered up to 80 tonnes of bombs, amounting to no fewer than 320 250 kg bombs dropped in just 54 sorties.

The main targets of the Russian 'Frogfoots' during this little-known, but fierce and bloody, local conflict were Islamist rebel groups infiltrating into Tajikistan from neighbouring Afghanistan by crossing the Pyandj River and then heading off via a number of mountain passes to fight all over the country. These passes became the prime targets of numerous aerial mine-laying missions using KMGU-2 mine dispensers. These weapons proved to be effective in disrupting the movement of enemy re-supply convoys and manpower reinforcements.

The Su-25s flying combat missions in Tajikistan were armed at all times with a pair of R-60 AAMs for self-defence in case they encountered Afghan fighter aircraft with hostile intentions either in Tajikistani airspace or in the disputed border areas. In the event no such encounters were reported during the entire 'hot' phase of the conflict, or in the years that followed.

RuAF Su-25s continued to see combat in 1994, with 116 strike and 171 reconnaissance sorties being flown totalling 617 flying hours. During the course of 1994 the Russian forces in Tajikistan were re-designated as peacekeepers, although the Su-25s' main mission remained unchanged. 186th IShAP's detachment continued its operations until 20 July 1994, after which personnel from other RuAF attack regiments were rotated in on temporary deployments to provide a long-term air power presence in the troubled region.

The second RuAF combat unit to be deployed to Tajikistan was Krasnodar-based 461st ShAP, which arrived at Kokayty in July 1994. Because of the limited number of protective flares carried by the Su-25Ks that equipped 461st ShAP during the unit's initial combat missions in Tajikistan, SAB-100 illumination bombs were employed for protection against the rebels' heat-seeking SAMs. Their use was eventually discontinued when stocks became exhausted. From then on Su-25 pilots were forced to eject flares in individual salvoes upon pressing the trigger to drop bombs or unleash rockets, as they remained the only available method of protection against heat-seeking shoulder-launched SAMs.

According to 461st ShAP pilot Mikhail Pavlov, the longest-range missions during his first deployment in Tajikistan in 1994 were flown to knock out targets in the Khorog Pass, some 180 miles from Kokayty. The Su-25s were equipped with two 800-litre external fuel tanks, and each aircraft carried a warload of six FAB-500M62 HE bombs plus two R-60 missiles. The flight to the target area and back was performed at a cruise altitude of 22,600 ft, and the ordnance was released on the pre-planned targets in one pass only. By the time they landed back at Kokayty all of the aircraft in the group were running on emergency fuel.

In mid-1995 the RuAF attack detachment operating in Tajikistan, consisting of ten aircraft (six single-seaters and four two-seaters), was relocated to Dushanbe-Aini airfield in Tajikistan. It continued its regular COIN operations from here for several more years. 18th GShAP 'Normandya-Neman', home-based at Galyonki, in Russia's Far East, sent a detachment to Dushanbe-Aini in August 1995 to replace 461st ShAP's detachment,

899th ShAP, home-based at Buturlinovka, saw its second combat deployment during the civil war in Tajikistan between 2 March and 16 December 1996, operating from Dushanbe-Aini airfield and performing 154 combat sorties. As this photograph illustrates, the unit's combat-weary Su-25s displayed large wavy-edged Russian tricolour flags during the deployment (*Andrey Zinchuk via Author*)

and it flew combat missions until August 1996. During the regiment's first war deployment the detachment performed 145 combat sorties, including 55 dedicated to attacking ground targets.

The second deployment of the Buturlinovka-based attack regiment (formerly 186th IShAP, but now re-designated as 899th ShAP) to Tajikistan took place between 2 March and 16 December 1996. As many as 154 combat sorties were flown from Dushanbe-Aini, 133 of these being dedicated to attacking ground targets and 21 to aerial reconnaissance. The 'Frogfoots' also escorted the Russian Army's tactical combat groups, each of which consisted of up to 30 armoured vehicles, during their movements and patrols in high-risk areas.

In the late 1990s and early 2000s a detachment of five aircraft and 50 air- and groundcrew was maintained at Dushanbe-Aini all year round. The operation saw the repeated rotation of personnel by three RuAF attack regiments, namely 266th ShAP, home-based at Step in Eastern Siberia, 187th ShAP, home-based at Chernigovka in Russia's Far East and 18th GShAP from Galyonki, also in Russia's Far East.

During the early 2000s Russian combat operations against the armed opposition in Tajikistan continued, albeit at a considerably lower intensity. In 2000, for instance, the deployed Su-25 force reported 45 combat sorties, but there were no attacks against ground targets and only show-of-force missions were flown. In 2001 the number of combat sorties flown by the detachment had dropped to 27, in 2002 it was 30 and in 2003 the figure fell to only three.

Two Su-25s were reported to have been lost since the beginning of the deployment, in 1998 and 2005, but both of these were written off in non-combat-related accidents. The first loss, on 11 April 1998, was an Su-25UB two-seater, with both pilots being killed when the aircraft hit the ground during a training mission over a mountainous area some 99 miles south of Tajikistan's capital, Dushanbe. The second 'Frogfoot' was lost in May 2005 when the pilot of Su-25BM '32', Maj Vladimir Pryadchenko of 899th ShAP, reported an in-flight fire and ejected successfully before the aircraft hit the ground about 15.5 miles from Dushanbe.

Since 23 October 2003 the RuAF's permanent detachment responsible for combat operations in Tajikistan, and all the other former Soviet republics in the region fighting against radical Islamist groups, has been stationed at Kant, in the former Soviet republic of Kyrgyzstan, within the structure of the 201st Russian Military Base.

A four-strong Su-25 detachment has been maintained within the structure of the 201st Russian Military Base in Kyrgyzstan since October 2003, manned on a rotational basis by aircrews from the attack regiments at Chernigovka, Galyonki and Step. The detachment is responsible for providing air support to Russian forces in Tajikistan and the other former Soviet republics in Central Asia, fighting radical Islamic movements and drug traffickers. This Su-25 of 187th ShAP, armed with B8M1 rocket pods, was photographed in July 2004 after landing at Kant air base (*Andrey Zinchuk via Author*)

CHAPTER SIX

CHECHNYA AND SOUTH OSSETIA

The RuAF 'Frogfoot' community, by now considered combat-hardened, was called into action again in 1994, this time in the breakaway Russian republic of Chechnya. This newly established territorial subject of the Russian Federation was born following the disintegration of the Chechnyan-Ingushetia Autonomous Soviet Republic in June 1992, just after the Ossetian-Ingushetian inter-ethnical conflict. Named the Chechen Republic of Ichkeria, it unilaterally declared its sovereignty and independence from the Russian Federation in 1993. The president of the new state was former VVS Maj Gen Dzhokhar Dudaev. In the summer of 1994 Russian-backed opposition groups attempted to remove Dudaev from power and install a Moscow-friendly government, but this plan reportedly failed to materialise.

Refusing to recognise the independence of the breakaway republic of Chechnya, the Russian government instead despatched troops to restore constitutional order in November 1994. By then the breakaway republic had become a 'criminal country destabilising the entire North Caucasus region inside the borders of the Russian Federation', according to the Kremlin. The ill-fated and extremely bloody military operation to remove Dudaev from power and return Chechnya to Russian rule officially started on 1 December 1994, but the massed bombings of Chechen airfields, where a great many L-29 and L-39C jet trainers were parked, by Su-25s had begun a few days earlier.

The three attack regiments of 1st GShAD, namely 368th ShAP at Budennovsk, 461st ShAP at Krasnodar and, later, 16th ShAP at Taganrog, bore the brunt of the operations during the campaign. Initially, 461st ShAP from Krasnodar was called upon to deploy its two squadrons, totalling 28 aircraft, to Budennovsk airfield. Each of these units was equipped with 12 single-seaters and two two-seaters, while 368th ShAP (already based at Budennovsk) deployed to Mozdok, in nearby Dagestan. In addition, a detachment from 899th GShAP from Buturlinovka was despatched to fly combat sorties over Chechnya, initially being deployed to Mozdok between 9 December 1994 and 21 January 1995 and then also moving to Budennovsk from 14 May to 16 June 1996.

Tasked with flying mostly CAS missions, the Su-25s undertook battlefield interdiction, destroyed enemy aircraft parked on airfields in Chechnyan territory and attacked weapons, ammunition storage depots and temporary bridges, as well as any other targets of military significance. The 'Frogfoot' pilots were also routinely tasked with conducting visual aerial reconnaissance sorties.

Maj Gen Viktor Bondaryov was CO of 899th ShAP during the Chechen campaigns. In April 2000, he was awarded the Golden Star of Hero of the Russian Federation (seen here hanging next to his right epaulette) for his combat and leadership achievements in both wars. He was appointed RuAF Commander-in-Chief in May 2012 and subsequently promoted to lieutenant general (*Andrey Zinchuk via Author*)

The Su-25s were instrumental in the destruction of the Presidential Palace in Grozny. Situated right in the centre of the city, the building boasted a reinforced concrete structure that had been turned into a well-defended fortress by the Chechens. Air power was viewed as a critical asset in the storming of the palace by Russian ground forces, Su-25s attacking it with S-24 rockets and BEtAB-500 concrete-piercing bombs on 17 and 18 February 1995. The bombs penetrated all floors from the roof to the basement, where Chechen forces had established a C^2 centre. The resulting explosions inflicted significant damage. After two days of heavy bombing by Su-25s (reportedly 899th ShAP aircraft), the Chechen combatants were forced to abandon the unsafe and heavily damaged palace and continue their fierce resistance from other parts of the city.

On 17 and 18 February 1995 the Presidential Palace in Grozny, which had been turned into a massive fortress by Chechen rebels, came under heavy attack by RuAF Su-25s armed with BEtAB-500 concrete-piercing bombs and S-24 rockets. They inflicted significant damage on the palace's structure, some of the bombs even penetrating through all of the floor levels from the roof to the basement, where Chechen forces had established a command-and-control centre (*RuAF via Author*)

Between October 1994 and September 1996 (a month after the Khasav-Yurt Accord finally brought a halt to the conflict) the RuAF's 'Frogfoot' force, consisting of 40 to 50 aircraft at any given time, carried out no fewer than 7000 combat sorties in-theatre totalling just over 7000 combat flying hours. Of these, 5828 sorties and 5756 hours were credited to the three regiments of 1st GShAD. About 3000 pre-planned strikes were reported by the 'Frogfoot' force, as well as 1115 CAS, 1284 free-hunting and no fewer than 500 aerial reconnaissance sorties. Nearly 20,000 unguided bombs were dropped, in addition to more than 100 RBK-250 cluster bombs, 69 KMGU-2 mine dispensers and 73,499 rockets of various calibres.

1st GShAD reported 23 instances of in-flight damage to its Su-25s, inflicted by heavy machine guns (four), AAA (five) and small-arms fire (14) during the first Chechen war campaign, the vast majority of these occuring below 2300 ft. Two Su-25s were lost in combat in 1995, with Capt Nikolay Bairov of 368th ShAP being killed in action on 4 February after a successful ejection – his jet was gunned down by a ZSU-23-4 mobile AAA system. On 5 May a second 368th ShAP Su-25 was reported lost after taking DhK-12.7 heavy machine gun hits during an attack on ground targets near the village of Benoi. Its pilot, Lt Col Vladimir Sarabeev, also perished in action.

Two more Su-25s were reported lost in 1996. The first of them was downed by a ZU-23 twin-barrel 23 mm AAA piece on 4 April near Toiskoe village. Its pilot, Capt Matveev of 368th ShAP, managed to eject, only to then become engaged in a firefight with Chechen combatants trying to capture him. He was eventually recovered at the last possible moment by a C-SAR party. The second aircraft loss was reported on 5 May when an Su-25UB two-seater, again from 368th ShAP, was brought down by a shoulder-launched SAM near Urus-Martan during a pre-planned strike. Pilots Col Igor Sviridov and Maj Oleg Isaev were both killed in action.

Alexander Koshkin, initially 1st AE CO and subsequently Deputy CO of 461st ShAP, flew no fewer than 200 combat sorties in the first Chechen war. In late 1995 he was tasked with destroying a D-30 122 mm howitzer, which he eventually detected hidden in an abandoned farm nine miles east of Grozny, not far from the city of Argun. After a 20-minute search he spotted the tracks of the howitzer's towing truck in the fresh snow a few kilometres from the initial search point (this was confirmed by a reconnaissance party sent to verify the post-strike results), and he then attacked the farm;

'I ordered my wingman to attack the T-shaped building [farmhouse] from a northern direction, while I made my strafing pass from the west. After the first hits the target became engulfed in black smoke, which usually appears when diesel fuel or engine oil is set ablaze.'

After pounding the howitzer hidden in the farm, Koshkin was urgently sent to the Gudermes area to seek out and destroy a BM-21 Grad multiple rocket launcher that had just fired on Russian troops. The two Su-25s quickly reached the target area, next to a railway station. Koshkin ordered his wingman to circle at 14,750 ft while he continued the visual search for the truck-mounted launcher, flying as low as 80 ft above the terrain. During his third turn over the area he spotted something resembling the nose of a Grad truck housed in an arched shelter. Koshkin decided to make a fourth turn so as to look over the shelter once more, passing abeam to clearly see the vehicle head-on. He then commenced an attacking manoeuvre before strafing the target with his cannon from a shallow dive angle. At that moment his Su-25 was hit in one of its engines by a large-calibre heavy machine gun round, setting it alight. Koshkin reacted immediately, activating the fire suppression system;

'I started turning towards the Terek River, ready to eject should the engine fire prove impossible to extinguish. Luckily the fire suppression system worked as advertised, and my Su-25 continued flying on one engine, maintaining a speed of 280 mph. I was unable to climb out, however, and at only 1300 ft the slow and low-flying Su-25 presented a very attractive target for the enemy on the ground. At last I managed to coax my damaged aircraft over the Terek River, exiting hostile territory. I then started feeling a little more relaxed, reporting the precise position of the Grad launcher that I had started to attack to the C^2 centre. After I had landed, the groundcrew discovered that my Su-25 had taken a hit from a 14.5 mm bullet [fired by a KPVT heavy machine gun], which punctured a tube in the engine's oil system. The leaking oil dripped onto the hot jetpipe, starting a fire.'

COIN TACTICS IN CHECHNYA

The pre-planned strikes in both Chechen wars were undertaken by two or three Su-25 pairs, attacking the targets at 30-minute intervals, while another pair of jets was always kept on quick reaction alert at Mozdok to reinforce the strike package whenever needed, or to provide on-demand CAS to troops in contact. A single Su-25 with a mixed war load of bombs and rockets was also kept as a spare, ready for immediate scramble in an emergency.

The typical combat workload comprised one or two sorties a day per pilot, but during the most intensive periods of fighting, when ground forces requested CAS all the time, 'Frogfoot' pilots logged up to five sorties a day.

When approaching a target area the Su-25 pairs usually flew at a cruising altitude of between 12,500 ft and 16,730 ft. The attack commenced with a roll in, the jet entering into a dive of between 45 and 60 degrees for accurate bomb drops and rocket firings. The ASP-17BTs-8 electro-optical sight was used in the manual aiming mode only, without any automatic corrections, while the Klyon-PS laser designator/rangefinder was not employed at all owing to significant ranging errors when the system was used over mountainous terrain.

Typically, the lead pilot would roll in first while his wingman remained at a safe altitude, circling overhead and looking at the ground for any muzzle flashes and launched SAMs. In the event of threats popping up, the wingman was to issue a prompt warning to the leader and then immediately roll in to attack the detected heavy machine gun/AAA emplacement(s) or SAM launch site(s). For the second attack cycle, the two aircraft switched roles, the wingman rolling in to attack and the leader providing top cover. The minimum pull-out altitude after a dive attack in which bombs had been dropped and/or rockets fired was set at 1970 ft, and this was reduced to 660 ft when strafing with the cannon.

SECOND CHECHEN CAMPAIGN

Officially conducted between August 1999 and April 2002, when the military phase of what had become a counter-terrorist operation was terminated, the second campaign in the troubled republic of Chechnya presented many challenges to the ailing Russian military machine. The RuAF attack force again played a vital role in supporting ground forces as they occupied the key cities in the republic, then continued to assail the remaining combat-capable Chechen units hiding in the mountains.

In August 1999 the campaign was initially proclaimed to be a large-scale anti-terrorist operation, aimed at repulsing the Chechen irregular armed groups occupying a number of cities and villages in the neighbouring Russian republic of Dagestan. Following these battles, which lasted 45 days, a large-scale rolling ground offensive was launched from four directions on 1 October 1999 towards the Chechen capital, Grozny. This offensive eventually led to the seizure of the city in January 2000. However, the Chechen armed opposition enjoyed the support of the local population and retreated into the mountains, mainly in the Argun and Vedeno valleys, where it switched to guerrilla warfare tactics and continued the organised resistance for a while.

The largest 'Frogfoot' strike of the second war was performed on 27 September 1999, just four days before the launch of the Russian ground offensive. Involving aircraft from all three regiments of 1st GShAD, as many as 60 Su-25s gathered at Mozdok were scrambled in a single wave and in complete radio silence. They were tasked with mounting a devastating pre-planned strike against a large number of important targets in Chechnya, mainly the airfields at Khankala, Kalinovskaya and Grozny North, as well as all known storage facilities with heavy military equipment. The main weapons used in this massed strike were rockets with armour-piercing warheads and HE bombs.

The first loss of the second Chechen War had been reported earlier that month, on 9 September. A 'Frogfoot' belonging to 960th ShAP suffered a double engine failure while attacking targets in the Karamakhi area of Dagestan with rockets. The pilot decided not to try to restart the engines, instead choosing to glide his un-powered Su-25 as far away from the target area as possible. He then ejected at low altitude and was promptly recovered by a C-SAR party. On 3 October another Su-25, this time belonging to 368th ShAP, was lost near Tolstoi-Urt due to enemy AAA. Its pilot, Capt Andrey Khmelevsky, was killed.

The biggest C-SAR operation during the second campaign in Chechnya was launched on 13 December when Col Sergey Borisuk, CO of 368th ShAP, was brought down. According to some sources his Su-25BM was hit by a shoulder-launched SAM while attacking targets in the Bachi-Urt area of the Argun Valley, whilst others claim the aircraft was downed by a defective

The upgraded Su-25SM, operated by one squadron within 368th ShAP from Budennovsk, saw its combat debut in the war in South Ossetia. The SM upgrade introduced the sophisticated PrNK-25SM integrated digital nav/attack suite, with a navigation accuracy for weapons delivery said to be within 46 ft using satellite correction, and 660 ft without it. The combination of the new head-up display, a weapons computer and the nav/attack system's digital components promised significantly increased accuracy (advertised as being between two to three times greater) when using unguided ordnance compared to the standard Su-25 (*Andrey Zinchuk via Author*)

122 mm rocket that exploded inside the B13L five-round pack beneath the wing of the jet.

After an uneventful parachute descent following his successful ejection, Borisuk became involved in a firefight with Chechen insurgents, who launched a large-scale search operation to capture him. He was eventually recovered by an Mi-8MT of the RuAF Flight Test Centre, but during the C-SAR operation, which lasted three days in enemy-controlled territory and involved Su-25s, Mi-24s and Mi-8MTs, Russian forces suffered painful losses, including two helicopters (one Mi-8MT and one Mi-24), six servicemen killed in action and six more badly wounded. Three more helicopters sustained significant damage from heavy machine gun and small-arms fire.

The first two attempts to recover Col Borisuk on 13 December proved fruitless following the loss of the Mi-8MT and the Mi-24. Finally, on 15 December, the C-SAR team made a third attempt to rescue him, and this time their efforts were successful.

On 22 January 2000 another Su-25 on a combat mission took a SAM hit while pulling out from an attack, although on this occasion its pilot, Maj A Karmanov of 461st ShAP, managed to return to base with one engine knocked out.

The worst RuAF loss of the campaign occurred on 14 June 2001 following the scrambling of the Su-25 QRA pair at Mozdok after an unidentified Antonov An-2 biplane was spotted inside the Argun Valley, presumably supplying the insurgents with ammunition from nearby Georgia. Two pilots flying MiG-29s that had originally been scrambled to engage other targets in Chechen airspace refused to intercept the An-2 because of bad weather in the area. The Su-25 pair on alert at Mozdok were then despatched to continue the search for the biplane, despite being armed with air-to-ground ordnance – one 'Frogfoot' was carrying FAB-500 bombs and the other S-24 rockets!

The pair flew into the Argun Valley just below the cloud ceiling, and after failing to spot the An-2 the leader reported that he was aborting the mission. At the same time he ordered his wingman to commence his climb-out in an effort to avoid collision with the valley walls. The climb-out manoeuvre, however, was initiated too late, and soon after entering the cloud cover both Su-25s flew into the ground. Lt Col Yuriy Yakimenko (Hero of Russian Federation) and Capt Oleg Podsitkov were both killed. After six days of intensive searching the remains of the pilots and their aircraft were found 1.265 miles apart at an altitude of about 8200 ft some 7.5 miles south of the mountain village of Itum-Kale.

On 29 April 2002 another 368th ShAP aircraft was reported lost while attacking an insurgent base some 3.70 miles from Dishne-Vedeno village. It struck high ground in the Vedeno Valley after unleashing 80 mm rockets in a 40-degree diving attack, the jet's destruction almost certainly being caused by a handling mistake (another account says that a SAM was fired by the insurgents). The pilot, Maj Igor Bezryadin, did not eject and was killed upon impact.

Su-25 WEAPONS IN CHECHNYA

During the second Chechen campaign RuAF Su-25s were employed only in daylight hours, mostly in two-aircraft flights in clear weather. However, on at least one occasion they were called upon to provide CAS in bad weather when troops of the Pskov-based 76th Guards Airborne-Attack Division were ambushed in a mountainous area near Ulus-Kert. As Mikhail Pavlov recalled, the cloud ceiling on that particular day was 1150 ft, while the peak height of the mountains was 2710 ft above sea level. The attacking passes were initiated by using reference points on the ground, without visual contact with the targets, which were covered by clouds. Heavy S-24 rockets were fired just below the cloud base while in a shallow climb, in a bid to achieve area saturation on a mountain slope that was above the Su-25s, covered by dense clouds.

Free-hunting missions were only conducted by the most experienced 'Frogfoot' pilots, usually flying in pairs. At pre-mission briefings for such sorties pilots were given information about their assigned patrol area and the type of targets they could expect to be detect and then attack. Pavlov detailed some of the most memorable moments from these missions;

'During one free-hunting mission my pair found two BM-21 Grad 122 mm self-propelled multiple rocket launchers, and their subsequent destruction turned into a spectacular fireworks display. On another mission we spotted a column of fuel trucks on the move, and I rolled in to attack. However, a second before pulling the trigger I saw my target explode. Moments later a second truck burst into flames, followed by a third. It turned out that the same column had just been attacked from another direction by an Mi-24 pair flying very low and communicating on another frequency. We made contact with the helicopters and started clarifying who was who in the air, and so on. I ordered my wingman not to attack, descending first to have a look at the scene on the ground so as to better assess the situation. The green helicopters flying low against a green background had proved impossible to spot from above before we rolled in to attack.'

FAB-500M62 and FAB-250M62 HE bombs were used in large numbers during both campaigns, while more powerful ODAB-500PM fuel/air bombs were only occasionally employed, mainly to destroy insurgent bases in forested areas. All bombing and rocket firings were performed using the ASP-17BTs-8 sight in the manual aiming mode, and ordnance delivery accuracy, as Pavlov recalled, depended solely on the pilot's skills and experience.

S-24 and S-25 heavy rockets were also commonly used, while the S-13 122 mm rocket, fired from five-round B13L packs, was introduced in 2000. Pilots tended to comment that they were very happy with the S-13, as this new type of ordnance proved both powerful and accurate.

As Pavlov explained, the poor accuracy of the Su-25's navigation equipment was partly solved by 461st ShAP in 1999, just before the start of the second campaign in Chechnya, thanks to the purchase of two commercial-standard hand-held GPS receivers at the consumer electronics market in Krasnodar – they were paid for out of the regiment's cash fund. These GPS receivers were widely used by the Su-25 pilots in combat sorties, although it was not publicly admitted that they had been the regiment's primary navigation tool because the unit lacked formal approval for their use by higher command. The GPS receiver proved to be very useful, accurately calculating all the necessary navigation information such as current position, distance to target,

Two Su-25Ts of the Lipetsk-based 4th TsPLSiBP, forward-deployed to Mozdok, were used to knock out high-value targets during the second Chechnya campaign, mainly using Kh-25ML and Kh-29L laser-guided missiles. They performed 39 combat sorties in total (*U-UAZ via Author*)

time to target and deviation from the pre-planned course. It also allowed the Su-25 group to meet the assigned time-on-target precisely by varying the speed of the aircraft while en route.

The RuAF Su-25s operating from Mozdok during both campaigns conducted their strike missions against targets in Chechnya that were usually up to 90 miles from their airfield, with an average sortie duration of one hour and five minutes to one hour and 15 minutes. All of the sorties were flown with two 800-litre external fuel tanks fitted, while a typical war load consisted of four to six S-24 or S-25 rockets, or a similar number of FAB-500 HE bombs, depending on the nature of the assigned targets.

During the second campaign in Chechnya, between August 1999 and July 2002 (technically, all fighting had 'ceased' at the end of April 2002, although RuAF assets remained in action until the early summer), the Su-25 force flew more than 7500 combat sorties. 368th ShAP completed 3726 combat sorties and logged 3814 flying hours, 461st ShAP's combat activity amounted to 2469 sorties totalling 2313 flying hours and for 960th ShAP those figures were 901 sorties and 906 flying hours, respectively.

In total, during both campaigns in Chechnya, the three Su-25 regiments of 1st GShAD flew 13,848 combat sorties totalling 13,319 flying hours.

Su-25T IN ACTION

In late 1999 two Su-25Ts drawn from Lipetsk-based 4th TsPLSiBP (*Ekipazh samoleta konversii i boyevoy podgotovki Tsentr* – Combat Training and Aircrew Conversion Centre) were deployed to Mozdok to mount strikes using precision-guided weapons. Subsequently performing 39 combat sorties, they destroyed a number of high-value targets in Chechnya such as a satellite communications facility, a radio relay station, the fortified house of well-known Chechen field commander Shamil Bassaev, a hangar housing defence equipment and, curiously, an An-2 light transport biplane on the ground that was suspected of ferrying weapons from nearby Georgia on 25 September 1999.

The principal weapons employed by the Su-25T pair in Chechnya were Kh-29L and Kh-25ML laser-guided missiles, but KAB-500L laser-guided and ODAB-500PM 500 kg FAE bombs were occasionally used to destroy underground shelters and weapons arsenals.

FIVE-DAY WAR

The war in South Ossetia in August 2008 was triggered by a Georgian Army attack launched in the late evening of 7 August and the early morning of 8 August against the capital city of the tiny breakaway province of South Ossetia. This, in turn, led to a prompt and excessively hard-hitting Russian military intervention.

The RuAF's 368th ShAP, stationed in Budennovsk, not far from South Ossetia, received an alert order at midnight on 7 August. By the early hours of the next day the CO, Col Sergey Kobilash, had received the mission tasking for his unit directly from the RuAF Commander-in-Chief, Col Gen Alexander Zelin. The regiment despatched two four-aircraft flights to South Ossetia in an effort to provide much-needed air support for the Russian peacekeeping forces stationed in the capital of the breakaway province, Tskhinvali, which at that time was being heavily shelled by the Georgian Army.

The four Su-25s of the formation led by Col Kobilash were the first RuAF aircraft to appear over the battlefield around Tskhinvali. Using the element of surprise, the 'Frogfoot' pilots flew a series of devastating low-altitude strafing passes on a Georgian Army military vehicle column, unleashing 80 mm rockets. The leaders of each pair in the RuAF formations were flying upgraded Su-25SMs (taken on strength in 2007-08) that boasted far better sighting and navigation equipment, while their wingmen had ordinary (non-upgraded) Su-25BMs.

Initially, the most important mission for RuAF Su-25s was battlefield air interdiction (BAI), which saw pilots called upon to mount strikes aimed at cutting off the flow of reinforcements and munitions heading from Georgia to the war zone in South Ossetia. For example, at midday on 8 August Kobilash and his wingman attacked a column belonging to the elite 4th Brigade of the Georgian Army that was moving from the city of Gori towards Tskhinvali. This attack resulted in the destruction of five trucks and several four-wheel drive vehicles, plus 20 Georgian soldiers reportedly killed (including a battalion CO from the 4th Brigade). A similar number were wounded.

Despite this successful mission, the opening 72 hours of the war saw Russian forces suffer losses both on the ground and in the air to friendly fire. It was reported that RuAF Su-25s attacked their own forces and South Ossetian irregulars on several occasions, and that the 'Frogfoots' were in turn targeted by RuAF MiG-29 fighters. Furthermore, Russian troops fired at everything in the air above Tskhinvali and adjacent areas. Veteran pilots who fought in both Chechen conflicts commented that the 'short and sharp' war in South Ossetia will be remembered for the very poor coordination between the 'Frogfoot' units and forces on the ground, at least at the beginning of combat operations.

The Su-25s from Budennovsk continued flying CAS and BAI sorties around Tskhinvali in the late afternoon hours of the critical first day (8 August) of the war. It was during this period that 368th ShAP suffered its first loss when Su-25BM '55', flown by Lt Col Oleg Terebunskiy (a veteran of both Chechen wars, with 120 combat sorties to his credit), was hit by a shoulder-launched SAM – the weapon was probably fired by South

Col Sergey Kobilash, CO of 368th ShAP, was in action from the very beginning of the South Ossetian campaign, flying an upgraded Su-25SM. Shot down over the southern suburbs of Tskhinvali on 9 August 2008, he successfully ejected and was promptly recovered by his own forces (*Russia TV via Author*)

The remains of Su-25BM '55', flown by Lt Col Oleg Terebunskiy during the South Ossetian campaign. Terebunskiy, a Chechen wars veteran with 120 combat sorties to his credit, ejected at about 1800 hrs on 8 August 2008 after his 'Frogfoot' took a hit, probably from a shoulder-launched Igla SAM fired by South Ossetian militants (*Author's collection*)

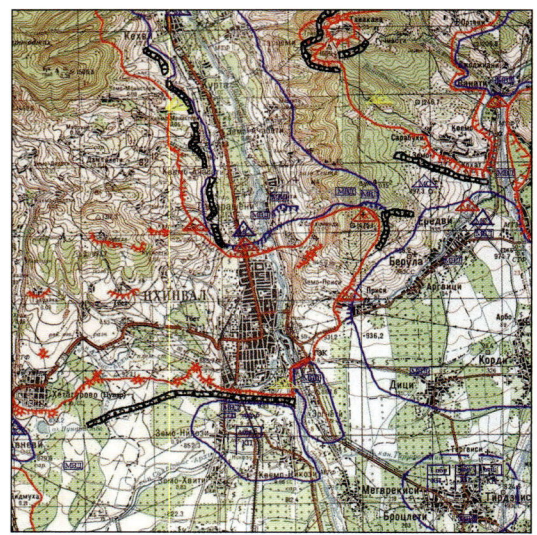

An original Russian-language map of the battlefield in South Ossetia in 2008 during the brief, but bloody, five-day war. In the centre of the map is the city of Tskhinvali, with the location of Russian forces on 9 August 2008 marked in red, and those of the Georgian forces in blue (*Author's collection*)

The remains of the Su-25BM flown by Maj Vladimir Edamenkov of 368th ShAP is inspected by a Russian ordnance disposal team tasked with destroying the jet's unexploded rockets after the end of the South Ossetian war. Edamenkov was killed in action when his Su-25 was shot down, probably by friendly fire, near the Gufta Bridge, the Su-25BM crashing into a forest near Itrapis village on 9 August 2008 (*Russian Ministry of Emergency Situations via Author*)

Ossetian irregulars. Terebunskiy was circling in the area between Dzhava and Tskhinvali at about 1800 hrs, attacking columns on the ground between Dzhava and Tskhinvali, when his aircraft was shot down. Another version of the incident states that Terebunskiy was shot down by an AAM mistakenly fired by a Russian fighter patrolling the area. Whatever the cause of his demise, the 'Frogfoot' pilot successfully bailed out and, although he was fired at with small arms by South Ossetian irregulars while descending and was wounded upon landing, he eventually managed to reach his own ground forces.

That same afternoon a pair of Su-25s led by Lt Col Vladimir Zvenigorodskiy (then deputy CO (Flight Training) of 368th ShAP) mounted a surprise attack against Marneuli airfield, the main GeAF jet base, some 13 miles south of the capital, Tbilisi. The 'Frogfoots' were virtually unopposed, with no SAM launches or AAA fire being reported during by the pair as they fired 80 mm rockets at targets inside the base. It later transpired that three An-2 light transports had been destroyed in the strike.

From dawn on day two (9 August) of the conflict, 368th ShAP continued its unsung and rather dangerous CAS and BAI work at low level in and around Tskhinvali. It was not long before the regiment reported its second loss, this time the downed pilot being Col Sergey Kobilash himself. He was on a mission to attack targets south of Tskhinvali when his Su-25SM was hit in the port engine by a shoulder-launched missile after he had pulled out from his third attack pass. The aircraft remained flyable for a period, and Kobilash tried his best to return the heavily damaged 'Frogfoot' to base despite the port engine being inoperable. This became a mission impossible when the slow-flying jet took another SAM hit, this time in the starboard engine, while overflying the South Ossetian-held southern suburbs of Tskhinvali. Kobilash had no choice other than to eject from about 3300 ft.

After an uneventful parachute descent into the middle of the Georgian-populated village of Dzartsemi, Kobilash had the good fortune to be promptly recovered by a C-SAR party consisting of a Mi-8MTV and a Mi-24P from 487th OVP BU (Independent Helicopter Regiment Combat and Control), also home-based at Budennovsk.

The second 'Frogfoot' to go down that day, and the third of the war, was reported in the late afternoon of 9 August. It was the lead aircraft of a pair from 368th ShAP tasked with escorting a Russian motorised column advancing from the Roki tunnel towards Dzhava and Tskhinvali. According to the wingman's account, while patrolling over the strategic road the Su-25 pair was mistakenly intercepted by two RuAF MiG-29s, the fighter pilots thinking that they had engaged GeAF attack aircraft. The 'Frogfoots' immediately began flying defensively, and while performing the scissors manoeuvre in an effort to escape from the fighters, the wingman, Capt Sergey Sapilin, saw the lead Su-25 take a head-on hit from a SAM or AAA fire. Its pilot, Maj Vladimir Edamenkov of 368th ShAP, failed to eject from the uncontrollable aircraft and was killed when his Su-25 hit the ground near the village of Itrapis.

It is noteworthy that all three downed 'Frogfoots' and most of the RuAF Su-25s damaged in the war are believed to have been hit by friendly fire, either from Russian troops or from South Ossetian irregulars firing Igla shoulder-launched missiles. In the case of Maj Edamenkov, it seems most likely that he was brought down by a Russian Army ZSU-23-4 self-propelled AAA system.

On 9 August another Su-25-equipped regiment, 461st ShAP, home-based at Krasnodar, joined the battle, deploying to Budennovsk and Mozdok. It ended the war without having suffered any losses, although one of its jets was badly damaged whilst being flown by Maj Ivan Konukhov. Flying as a pairs lead, he and his wingman had taken off from Budennovsk at 1120 hrs on 11 August to perform a CAS mission. Loitering at medium altitude waiting to be assigned a task by a ground-based FAC, the pair was finally ordered to attack a concentration of Georgian vehicles loaded with ammunition that were parked near the village of Zemo Nikozi, not far from the war-torn city of Tskhinvali. Konukhov rolled in for the first pass on the vehicles and then repeated the attack, although this time he fired rockets at a nearby wood in which Georgian combatants had taken shelter.

While pulling out from the last attack Konukhov's Su-25K suffered a powerful hit in the starboard engine. The SAM warhead detonated next to the aircraft, causing a total engine failure and subsequent fire. The latter in turn destroyed the hydraulic and electrical systems, rendering most of the instruments in the cockpit useless. Konukhov immediately carried out his emergency drill, as he later recalled;

'I performed all the actions required of me by the flight manual when faced with such an emergency situation, the first of which was activating the fire suppression system, which worked as advertised and stopped the fire. Within seconds my speed had dropped down to 135-140mph and the aircraft was barely able to maintain level flight. Having lost sight of my wingman, I found myself flying over a featureless terrain, with inoperative navigation equipment on board. I felt despair at my plight, as my aircraft had been rendered blind, nothing worked and nobody replied to my calls for help over the radio.'

Konukhov continued navigating by using the sun, which was the only available reference. It was midday, and the sun was to the south, so he turned directly north and flew for one hour towards the airfield. He had decided that ejection was not an option, and he eventually succeeded in overflying the main Caucasus ridgeline, his damaged aircraft stalling twice owing to a loss of speed while trying to climb over the mountains. Konukhov eventually managed to reach Mozdok, where he landed on emergency fuel, with enough kerosene in the tanks for only a few more minutes of flight.

Two more Su-25s from 368th ShAP were also heavily damaged, although their pilots, Capt Ivan Nechaev and Col Oleg Molostov, managed to bring their 'Frogfoots' home. Molostov's Su-25SM, '08', was holed in 88 places by fragments from a PZL Grom shoulder-launched

Su-25K '46' of 461st ShAP, flown by Maj Ivan Konukhov, was badly damaged by a shoulder-launched SAM on 11 August 2008 while performing a combat mission over South Ossetia. Konukhov managed to make an emergency landing at Mozdok (*Author's collection*)

Upgraded Su-25SM '09' of 368th ShAP, flown by Capt Ivan Nechaev, was badly damaged by a SAM hit on 11 August 2008, although the pilot flew the 'Frogfoot' back to base. After the landing fuel was leaking from a punctured fuel line, so the tarmac beneath the aircraft was liberally covered with fire-suppressant foam (*Author's collection*)

SAM (a Polish licence-built version of the Russian 9K38 Igla system, Georgia having acquired 30 launchers and 100+ missiles) when the warhead detonated in close proximity during an attack on Georgian military vehicles near Mereti on 8 August. Molostov and his wingman, Capt Ivan Nechaev, reportedly destroyed ten Toyota pick-ups, two military trucks and one infantry fighting vehicle.

Around midday on 11 August Su-25SM '09', flown by Capt Ivan Nechaev of 368th ShAP, was said to have been targeted by five or six SAMs over the western end of Tskhinvali. They were fired shortly after the pilot had rolled in for a second attacking pass with 122 mm rockets. One of the SAMs hit the jet in the tail and then knocked out the port engine when its warhead detonated. The starboard engine also sustained some damage but continued to run, albeit at a reduced thrust rating. Some Russian researchers believe that Nechaev had mistakenly attacked a Russian military column, resulting in his aircraft being struck by an Igla SAM after ground troops believed that they were being attacked by a Georgian 'Frogfoot'.

All three heavily damaged Su-25s were subsequently sent to the 121st Aircraft Repair Plant at Kubinka, near Moscow, for examination. Here, they were judged to be beyond economical repair and subsequently withdrawn from use.

368th ShAP Su-25s reportedly flew about 100 combat sorties during the war. The first day of the conflict (8 August) was the most intense, with the vast majority of the available pilots flying three sorties each. This operational tempo enabled the RuAF to maintain a combat pair over the battlefield at any given time until the end of that critical day. 461st ShAP remained committed to the campaign for another three days after 8 August, flying 36+ combat sorties during that time.

Confusingly for troops on the ground, Su-25s were flown by both sides during the conflict – hence the numerous friendly fire incidents. The GeAF had ten Su-25s on strength when Georgia invaded South Ossetia, four of these jets being Su-25KM Scorpions that had been upgraded by Elbit Systems of Israel and four that were standard 'Frogfoots'. The GeAF was also equipped with a pair of Su-25U two-seaters.

Georgian Su-25s were only employed at the very start of the war when six aircraft were loaded with ordnance and their pilots briefed to attack the 58th Army armoured columns passing through the Roki tunnel during the early hours of 8 August. It was hoped that such a strike would slow the Russian advance towards the battlefield in Tskhinvali. In the event only four 'Frogfoots' (one Su-25KM and three standard jets) reportedly managed to take off from Marneuli and deliver their ordnance on an advancing Russian military column near the city of Dzhava – all of the 250 kg free-fall bombs that were dropped missed their intended targets, however. No losses were inflicted on the 58th Army as a result, this fact being confirmed by Russian journalists who were travelling with the column that was bombed by the GeAF.

According to Georgian sources no further combat missions were flown. All of the GeAF's Su-25s survived the war as a result, most if not all of them being well hidden beneath camouflage netting at Marneuli.

EXPORT Su-25s IN COMBAT

The war between Iran and Iraq was the second local conflict of the 1980s in which the Su-25 proved it could be an effective CAS workhorse, operating mainly at low altitude and facing a wide range of air-defence weapons. The Iraqi Air Force (IrAF) had been the first non-Eastern Bloc country to be officially briefed on the Su-25 in the Soviet Union, Iraqi officers being shown the aircraft in May 1986. In total, Iraq is reported by Russian sources to have acquired as many as 69 Su-25K single-seaters and four Su-25UBK two-seaters in two batches, ordered in 1986 and 1987, respectively. This quantity was sufficient to equip two ground-attack regiments.

An IrAF Su-25K lies destroyed on the ground after being hit by a laser-guided bomb during Operation *Desert Storm* in January 1991. This aircraft was caught in the open at Jalibah South-east airfield, which was captured by the US Army's 2nd Brigade, 24th Infantry Division on 27 February 1991 following a brief engagement with 1000 Iraqi troops and 20 tanks *(SSgt Dean Wagner/USAF)*

The 'Frogfoot' saw extensive use in the closing stages of the war with Iran, its fairly intensive employment again demonstrating the aircraft's admirable degree of battlefield survivability. On one occasion an Su-25K was even said to have survived a hit by an MIM-23 Hawk SAM missile – despite the jet being heavily damaged by the weapon's powerful warhead, its pilot managed to land the aircraft in one piece. Two Iraqi Su-25Ks were reportedly lost, however, while conducting combat missions during the war.

IrAF Su-25s were not used in anger during the 1991 Gulf War, their only known flying activity being the escape of nine aircraft to Iran – two of these jets were shot down by USAF McDonnell Douglas F-15Cs on 6 February 1991. A large number of Iraqi 'Frogfoots' were also destroyed inside their hardened aircraft shelters during Coalition air strikes, bunker-busting Paveway laser-guided bombs making short work of the jets. The

Although a number of IrAF 'Frogfoots' survived the carnage of *Desert Storm*, they saw very little use in the years prior to Operation *Iraqi Freedom* (OIF) in March 2003. This Su-25K was one of a handful of jets that were inexplicably buried under the sand at several air bases on the eve of OIF *(via Author)*

IrAF Su-25K 25616 (c/n 10310) as captured by US troops at the former Taqaddum air base (near Habbaniyah) during OIF. This aeroplane was one of several captured at the airfield that featured the 'Dome of the Rock' insignia beneath the cockpit, this marking having been applied prior to the jet's participation in a flypast that was part of a military parade staged in Baghdad on 31 December 2001. Note that someone has already 'souvenired' the IrAF marking from the jet's fin (*via Tom Cooper*)

handful of surviving IrAF Su-25Ks were buried under the sand at several air bases on the eve of Operation *Iraqi Freedom* in March 2003. Thus, the 'Frogfoot' did not represent any real threat to Coalition forces during their advance on Baghdad to overthrow President Saddam Hussein.

The National Air Force of Angola was another early Su-25 operator that saw combat with the 'Frogfoot'. A total of 12 single-seaters and a pair of two-seaters were delivered in early 1988 and taken on strength by a squadron within the 26th Fighter-Bomber Regiment, stationed at Namib airfield. The first training operations, under the supervision of VVS instructors, began in February 1989, and by August that year the squadron had two combat-ready flights, each consisting of four pilots.

Angolan aircrews began flying operational CAS sorties in late 1990, bombing UNITA armed opposition forces advancing towards the capital, Luanda. However, the Angolans' *modus operandi* for combat missions proved to be ill-suited to the Su-25 because, as Soviet military advisers recalled, they used the type as a bomber. Pilots dropped their ordnance (mainly OFAB-100-120 and OFAB-200-270 bombs) from 16,500 ft to 23,100 ft in level flight so as to stay out of reach of Stinger SAMs and AAA pieces operated by UNITA. Su-25s flew as many as 25 combat sorties during the campaign, but by March 1991 the regiment had lost its combat capability owing to a lack of serviceable aircraft following the withdrawal of Soviet support.

There are reports and photographic evidence to suggest that a small number of Su-25s were restored to airworthiness in 1993 and again operated in combat against UNITA until the following year. This time, however, mercenary pilots provided by South Africa's Executive Outcomes (EO), a private military company, were employed to fly the jets. They are known to have operated out of Saurimo airfield, tasked with supporting EO operations to seize diamond fields from the rebels.

Another local conflict in Africa in which the type was used in anger was the war between Ethiopia and Eritrea. In March 2000 the Ethiopian Air Force took on strength two former RuAF Su-25Ts upgraded to Su-25TK standard before delivery. These 'Super Frogfoots' were sold together with a pair of secondhand two-seaters, upgraded to Su-25UBK standard. Combat sorties were flown from bases at Debre Zeit and Mekele.

Manned by Ethiopian aircrew trained in Russia, the three surviving aircraft (one was written off shortly after its arrival in-country) took part in the closing stage of the war against Eritrea, which ended on

The National Air Force of Angola employed its Su-25Ks in late 1990 against UNITA forces, but they were soon grounded owing to the withdrawal of Soviet maintenance support. A small number of 'Frogfoots' are known to have been returned to airworthy condition in 1992-95 and again used in combat against UNITA, but this time the aircraft were flown by mercenary pilots from South African company Executive Outcomes (*Author's collection*)

10 June 2000. One Kh-29T TV-guided missile and two Kh-25ML laser-guided missiles were reportedly fired in combat by the Ethiopian pilots, who claimed that all of the weapons had hit their assigned targets – a number of S-24 240 mm rockets were also expended. The Kh-29T TV-guided missile was used to destroy a hardened shelter. An S-24-armed Su-25UBM also took part in an attack on an Eritrean SAM position in Mendefera, some 37 miles south of the capital, Asmara, on 21 May 2000, and then targeted the military training centre in Sava. Seventeen combat sorties were flown in three weeks of fighting, eight of them by Su-25TKs.

This Su-25 was one of three single-seaters and a solitary two-seater purchased from Ukraine by the former Yugoslavian Republic of Macedonia in 2001 as an urgent measure to cope with the uprising of ethnic Albanian separatists that had erupted in March of that year (*Chris Lofting*)

The fledging air arm of Macedonia took delivery of three ex-Ukrainian Su-25s and one Su-25UB two-seater, originally sourced from Belarus, in June 2001 under an urgent procurement programme. The newly acquired 'Frogfoots' were immediately used in anger against ethnic Albanian insurgents occupying a number of villages, the jets being flown by Ukrainian mercenary pilots. The Su-25s arrived after the culmination of the conflict, however, and reportedly fired their weapons on only one occasion – a sole 'Frogfoot' performed attacks using mainly 57 mm rockets against a T-55 main battle tank that had been captured by the insurgents, but without any success. The tank-hunting mission ended with no result.

Although seeing next to no combat, the newly delivered Macedonian 'Frogfoots' flew several visual reconnaissance and show-of-force missions over the insurgent-occupied villages.

Peru took delivery of 18 ex-Belarusian Su-25s in 1998, comprising ten late-build single-seaters and eight two-seaters, and shortly thereafter they saw use in anger in an innovative role – as interceptors of drug-trafficking aircraft. In 1999 and 2000 the Peruvian 'Frogfoots' were rushed into action to reinforce the nation's anti-drug campaign. The Su-25's good thrust-to-weight ratio allowed it to easily intercept general-aviation aircraft smuggling raw cocaine and cocaine paste from the Upper Hulanga Valley, in the northern part of Peru, into neighbouring Columbia. The first such shoot-down was claimed on 18 July 2000, in an area north of the capital, Lima. It is believed that at least 25 drug-carrying light aircraft were destroyed between 2000 and 2005.

Peru's air arm operated as many as ten single-seaters and eight two-seaters acquired from Belarus. This is one of the two-seaters upgraded for use in suppressing enemy air defences, using the Kh-58U anti-radar missile (ARM). The new avionics package comprised the L150 Pastel radar warning receiver/emitter locator system, with most of its black boxes, together with the launch control and target designation equipment of the ARM, housed in a KRK-UO underfuselage pod. The rear cockpit instrument panel was modified with an IM-3M-14 monochrome CRT display, on which target and launch control information derived from the Pastel and the ARM's seeker head was displayed (*Chris Lofting via Author*)

CHAPTER SEVEN

An impressive line up of 13 Su-25s and 12 Su-22s at Talara air base, in northern Peru, in April 2005. Although the 'Fitters' were retired in 2007, the 'Frogfoots' remain in service. However, only four of the 18 Su-25s supplied by Belarus in 1998 are presently believed to be serviceable (*Chris Lofting*)

The Democratic Republic of Congo received four factory-fresh Su-25s acquired from TAM in 1999-2000, and these were used in anger on several missions during the internal conflict in the country. Flown by mercenary pilots from the former Soviet republics, the Su-25s often carried 1500-litre external fuel tanks. This was the first time such large tanks had been fitted to the 'Frogfoot', having been introduced in-theatre to extend the jet's combat radius due to targets typically being some 300+ miles from base. The Su-25s conducted these long-range strikes laden with four 250 kg FAB-250M62 HE bombs, using a high-low-high mission profile.

Another 'Frogfoot' operator that gained notoriety in 2004 was the air arm of the Ivory Coast, which used its aircraft in action against anti-government forces during the Ivorian Civil War. At least four aircraft, two of which were two-seaters, were procured from Belarus in 2004 and based at Abidjan. The two-seaters, flown by mixed crews consisting of one local pilot and a Belarusian mercenary, were forward-deployed to Yamoussoukro airfield in late October or early November 2004, and soon afterwards began attacking anti-government forces in the town of Bouake. The first strikes were undertaken on 4 November and, two days later, the jets mistakenly targeted a French military camp – France has had troops in its former colony since the civil war started in September 2002, supporting the United Nations peacekeeping mission and ensuring the security of French and foreign nationals.

The Democratic Republic of Congo received four factory-fresh Su-25s acquired from TAM in 1999-2000, and these were saw combat on several missions during the internal conflict in the country. Flown by mercenary pilots from the former Soviet republics, the Su-25s routinely carry 1500-litre external fuel tanks, as seen here (*Melting Tarmac Images*)

Two jets flown by Belarusian mercenary pilots twice circled the camp before rolling in to unleash their 57 mm S-5 rockets. Nine French troops and a visiting American were killed, with 23 others injured. Later that same day both Su-25UBs were damaged beyond repair on the tarmac at Yamoussoukro by French Special Forces in an act of revenge. The remaining two Su-25s apparently shared the same fate, being badly damaged while parked in their hangar at Abidjan.

More recently, Su-25s have seen combat in Iran, where a fleet of three two-seaters and five single-seaters have been operational with the aviation arm of the Islamic Revolutionary Guard (IRG) since three newly built Su-25UBKs were delivered in 2004. The 'Frogfoot' fleet was reinforced shortly thereafter by the introduction of five ex-Iraqi Su-25Ks whose pilots fled to Iran in January 1991. These single-seaters had been returned to airworthy condition after spending between 13 and 15 years in storage.

On 1 November 2012 a pair of IRG 'Frogfoots' were reported to have intercepted and fired warning shots at a US MQ-1 Predator unmanned aerial vehicle (UAV) flying in international airspace over the Persian Gulf just outside the limit of Iran's 12-mile territorial waters and adjacent airspace. The Predator attacked by the 'Frogfoots' was on a routine surveillance mission at about 0450 hrs, 16 miles from the Iranian coastline. At least one of the Su-25 pilots opened fire at the Predator with his aircraft's twin-barrel 30 mm cannon, but no hits were reported and the drone turned away from the coastline, pursued by the IRG pilots, who fired another burst, which also missed, before disengaging.

Sudan is among the more recent Su-25 operators, having acquired 14 second-hand 'Frogfoots' from Belarus – 11 in 2008 and three more in 2009 – that were quickly sent into action following their arrival in-country. In 2013 it was revealed that another batch of Su-25s had been acquired, together with S-8 80 mm rockets fired from B8M1 20-round rocket

This aircraft was one of two Su-25UBs of the *Force Aerienne de Cote d'Ivoire* that carried out an S-5 rocket attack on a French military camp on 6 November 2004. Both jets (and two single-seat 'Frogfoots') were rendered inoperable by French Special Forces at Yamoussoukro airfield a few hours later, the soldiers firing Milan anti-tank guided missiles at the aircraft (*via Mark Lepko*)

All four badly damaged 'Frogfoots' of the *Force Aerienne de Cote d'Ivoire* were removed from the runway at Yamoussoukro airfield and placed in storage in a nearby hangar. Military officials from the Ivory Coast asked the United Nations for permission to repair and overhaul the aircraft in 2012, but this request was denied following pressure from the French government (*via Pit Weinert*)

Photographed in 2007 shortly after their return to airworthiness following 16 years in storage, these former IrAF Su-25Ks are presently assigned to the Iran Islamic Revolutionary Guards, whose distinctive unit emblem can be seen on the fins of both jets. The aircraft closest to camera carries an R-60 AAM on its outer underwing pylon. 15-2456 was returned to IrAF control on 30 June 2014 when three Su-25UBKs and four Su-25Ks were flown from Iran at short notice following ISIL's invasion of Iraq (*Farzad Bishop*)

packs. The number of aircraft involved in this latest purchase has not been confirmed, although it is believed that up to ten jets were delivered.

Sudanese military forces have been involved in a long-running internal conflict against insurgents in the nation's southern areas that finally resulted in the independence of South Sudan in July 2011. At the time of the jets' purchase the Sudanese government claimed that the Su-25s would not be used in the Darfur conflict, where civil war has been raging since 2003. In 2010 and 2011, however, there were a number of reports that the newly delivered Su-25s, together with other attack types, were being used to attack cities and villages in the troubled region. At the time the government claimed that the aircraft were being deployed to guard troops, and attributed the allegations of attacks on civilians to propaganda from opposition groups and their supporters. However, according to reports from Amnesty International, Sudanese Su-25s were involved in indiscriminate air strikes on 14 and 25 June 2011 in the region of Southern Kordofan, firing S-5 57 mm and S-24 240 mm rockets. The Su-25s used in these operations were reported to have been based at El-Obeid, in Northern Kordofan.

Sudan is numbered among the latest 'Frogfoot' operators, having purchased 14 former Belarusian Air Force Su-25s. These were delivered during 2008-09, and in 2013 the fleet was enlarged with the acquisition of ten more jets from the same source. These jets were photographed at Al-Fashir airport, in the Darfur region, between missions on 21 August 2011. They are armed with 20-round B8M1 pods for firing S-8 80 mm rockets (*Melting Tarmac Images*)

CURRENT CONFLICTS

The latest war in which the Su-25 has been used in anger is the bloody internal conflict in Ukraine that erupted in mid-April 2014. At the outbreak of large-scale military operations against the pro-Russian separatist militia forces that had initially managed to seize control over vast regions in the south-eastern part of this former Soviet Union republic, the Ukrainian Air Force (UkAF) had a fleet of about 70 'Frogfoots', but only 15 or so of these were considered to be in airworthy condition. However, during the first two months of the conflict another six to ten aircraft are reported to have been returned to service.

All of the Su-25s were flown by the 299th Tactical Aviation Brigade (TAB) based at Nikolayev-Kulbakino, and a number of the jets had been modified to M1 standard. The upgraded 'Frogfoot' M1 prototype flew for the first time in 2004, and it was formally commissioned into Ukrainian service in March 2010, at the same time as the first three upgraded and refurbished aircraft – two Su-25M1 single-seaters and one Su-25UBM1 two-seater – were taken on strength.

M1 jets have had a number of important components in the Su-25's original KN-23-1 navigation suite and the SUO-8-1 attack suite replaced, thus improving navigation and weapons delivery accuracy. In an effort to keep the costs involved with the upgrade as low as possible, no fuselage, cockpit or powerplant alterations were introduced. As many as nine upgraded single-seaters and one two-seater had been delivered to the 299th TAB up to early 2014. However, the UkAF struggled to find qualified pilots to fly the 'Frogfoots' at the start of the war because so few aviators had currency on the jet due to an acute shortage of flying hours caused by insufficient airworthy aircraft and frequent fuel shortages since the early 2000s.

The first use of UkAF Su-25s in anger was reported in mid April, the aircraft initially conducting show-of-force missions only over the separatist-held towns and villages in the Donetsk and Lugansk regions, supporting the initial push of the Ukrainian forces, including Army, Ministry of Interior/National Guard, Territorial Defence and Security Service units. Forward-deployed to Dnepropetrovsk airport, some 124 miles from Donetsk and 180 miles from Lugansk, Su-25s may have also used

This UkAF Su-25M1, displaying the latest-standard four-tone grey 'digital' camouflage, was one of ten upgraded 'Frogfoots' available for use in anger against the pro-Russian militant forces of the self-proclaimed Lugansk and Donetsk people's republics in the southeastern part of the country. The first combat sorties that saw the employment of ordnance against ground targets were reported at the beginning of May 2014. The weapons under the starboard wing of this aircraft are an OFAB-250M-54 250 kg general-purpose bomb and an S-25OFM rocket (*Chris Lofting via Author*)

CHAPTER EIGHT

Armed with four 20-round B8M1 pods and two OFAB-250M-54 250 kg bombs, and carrying 1500-litre external fuel tanks, a UkAF Su-25 goes in search of targets over eastern Ukraine in the summer of 2014 (*via Author*)

Pro-Russian separatists examine the remains of one of two UkAF Su-25s downed on 23 July 2014. The 'Frogfoots' were shot down by a separatist militia force, probably using Igla shoulder-launched missiles, near the Saur-Mogila hardened defensive position set up on a strategic hill in south-eastern Ukraine (A*uthor's archive*)

Chuguev airfield as a forward operating base.

The first appearance of the Su-25 in the war zone was reported on 15 April when a single aircraft was tasked with providing top cover for Ukrainian Army Aviation (UkAA) Mi-8MT transport helicopters delivering an assault party to seize the airfield near the city of Kramatorsk. The first 'hot' mission for the UkAF 'Frogfoot' force was reported on 5 May. Its aim was to destroy a UkAA Mi-24P attack helicopter that had made a forced landing well inside separatist-held territory, and thereby prevent capture of the helicopter's ordnance. The doomed Mi-24P was resting inside a swampy area not far from the breakaway city of Slavyansk – it took direct hits by S-8KO 80 mm rockets and was completely destroyed by the subsequent fire.

In mid and late May the Su-25 force continued its occasional operations over separatist-held territories, flying from Dnepropetrovsk and Chuguev airfields. Russian researchers of the conflict have suggested that the Su-25s involved were organised into the so-called Reserve Aviation-Attack Group, and in May and June no fewer than four of its 'Frogfoots' were spotted parked at Dnepropetrovsk airport.

Initially, Ukrainian Su-25s were only lightly armed when flying combat sorties, carrying only two 20-round B8M1 packs for firing S-8KO 80 mm rockets, a full ammunition load for the built-in cannon and two 800-litre external fuel tanks.

According to Igor Strelkov, the separatist force commander in the self-proclaimed Donetsk People's Republic, in the second half of June a number of 'Frogfoots' were forward deployed to the airfield at Mariupol, not far from the militia-held territories.

Late the previous month, on 26 May, UkAF Su-25s were involved in a successful operation against the separatists of the militia's Vostok battalion who had seized the terminal building at Donetsk airport, opening fire at it shortly after dawn and inflicting heavy casualties. The Su-25 pair performing this mission flew in a very careful manner, using protective flares to decoy the Igla shoulder-launched SAMs that were known to be in the separatist militia's arsenal – video footage on the internet shows at least one unsuccessful SAM launch against the attacking Su-25s. A militia training camp in the Lugansk region was also targeted by Su-25s in late May.

These attacks were flown against targets in the open, far from any urban environment. However, when the Su-25s were used to attack targets in cities (such as Lugansk, Slavyansk and Kramatorsk) they inflicted a significant amount of collateral damage and killed a number of civilians because they employed S-8 rockets – an area saturation weapon. This was precisely what happened on 2 June during the now notorious attack on the municipal government building in the city of Lugansk, which was used as the headquarters of the self-proclaimed People's Lugansk Republic. No fewer than eight S-8s are reported to have hit a park just in front of the building, killing seven civilians and wounding 28, while the target itself remained intact.

The Ukrainian government denied that there had been an airborne attack in the centre of Lugansk, but there was much evidence to the contrary, including video footage recorded by casual observers and security cameras installed in the centre of the city. The use of S-8 rockets launched from an aircraft against a target in the centre of Lugansk was also confirmed by observers from the Organisation for Security and Stability in Europe, who conducted a post-strike survey of the site.

During the fierce battles raging around the city of Slavyansk on 3 and 4 June the militants defending the breakaway city claimed an Su-25 shot down, but this has never been confirmed by independent sources.

The next instance of the successful use in anger of UkAF 'Frogfoots' was in the battle for checkpoint at Marinovka, on the Russian–Ukrainian border. In this engagement, on 5 June, a single Su-25 caught troops and vehicles of the Vostok battalion in the open, inflicting serious losses.

In mid-June the separatist militia claimed to have shot down an Su-25 that launched a rocket attack against the police station in the city of Gorlovka, occupied by the militants, killing four people. This happened in the early hours of 14 June, and the pilot managed to bail out and was captured. Again, there was no confirmation of this claim from independent sources. Another shoot-down claim was made by the separatists in Gorlovka three days later, and this time amateur video footage was released showing an attacking Su-25 pumping out protective flares and firing rockets that also appears to be hit by ground fire. Its final fate remains unknown, however, as the UkAF listed no losses for 17 June. Yet another Su-25 was claimed on 19 June, but its loss has not been confirmed by independent sources either.

On 28 June the UkAF 'Frogfoot' force was used in an unusual way in the combat zone – to deliver emergency supplies to Ukrainian airborne troops defending the besieged airfield at Kramatorsk and other locations in Donetsk. Several Su-25s were spotted performing this task, flying at medium altitude and reportedly dropping containers of food and medicines, which descended beneath parachutes. These containers, carried on the underwing pylons, were probably converted bodies of 250 kg illumination bombs. The vast majority of the drops failed to reach their intended targets, however, due to strong winds. The supplies were subsequently seized by the separatists.

After the ending of a temporary ceasefire observed by government forces from 21 June to 1 July, the UkAF 'Frogfoots' were seen in action again over the Kramatorsk area, attacking militant forces with rockets and, for the first time, iron bombs. Two 'Frogfoots' were claimed shot down on the 1st, but as in the previous cases in June, there was no confirmation from Ukrainian or independent sources. The UkAF did admit that one of its Su-25s had been damaged by heavy machine gun fire near Snezhnoe, however. Another 'Frogfoot' shoot-down claim was made on 2 July, and this time the Ukrainian authorities issued a press release stating that an Su-25 pilot had lost control while landing at Dnepropetrovsk airport following a combat sortie and been forced to eject.

An Su-25 bombing targets in rebel-held territory during the early afternoon of 16 July was reported to have sustained heavy damage, although its pilot managed to return to base. That evening another 'Frogfoot' was brought down by an Igla SAM in the Amvrosievka area, not far from the Russian border. Its pilot ejected safely. In the wake of this incident a Ukrainian security council spokesman accused Russia of shooting down the Su-25 with an air-to-air missile fired from a RuAF fighter. Yet another UkAF 'Frogfoot' was destroyed on 21 July while on a combat mission, its wreckage being discovered near the village of Marinovka, a short distance from Lugansk. The pilot of the jet, Lt Col Yury Shevtsov (a squadron CO from the 299th TAB) ejected safely and managed to avoid being captured for nearly a month. Eventually, he was arrested by the separatists and interrogated, before being released in a prisoner exchange between the warring parties.

On 23 July two Su-25s were brought down while bombing the militant stronghold at Saur-Mogila, near the Russian border east of Donetsk. The jets were part of a four-aircraft mission, and after they had been hit (probably by shoulder-launched missiles) their pilots ejected and managed to escape capture. The remains of one aircraft were found near the village of Dmitrievka and the wreckage of the second jet was located near the city of Shakhtyorsk. Ukrainian sources claimed that one of these Su-25s had fallen victim to a Russian fighter firing air-to-air missiles from across the border, but this accusation cannot be confirmed. The Russian government has also continued to deny any involvement in the conflict by RuAF fighters.

After the losses and damage sustained in some three months of combat, the UkAF continued conducting attack missions – at a significantly reduced tempo – with around ten surviving Su-25s during the autumn of 2014, mostly at high altitude above 16,400 ft so as to avoid being hit by shoulder-launched missiles. However, as the VVS had discovered in Afghanistan some three decades earlier, accuracy suffered in delivering weapons from such heights. On 26 August, a four-ship Su-25 formation was seen in amateur video footage attacking militant positions near Pervomaysk, 13 miles from the border with Russia. This time the 'Frogfoots' flew at relatively high altitude, maintaining high speed and dropping light-and-heat-emitting illumination bombs, which slowly descended on parachutes, as durable decoys for the infrared seeker heads of insurgent-launched SAMs.

Despite such precautions being taken, the UkAF suffered one more Su-25 loss, on 29 August. The sixth confirmed 'Frogfoot' loss of

Following the rise of the ISIL threat in northern and western Iraq during the summer of 2014, the IrAF took an urgent delivery of four or five ex-RuAF Su-25s that were transported to Baghdad International Airport by an An-124 military airlifter on 28 June (*Iraqi MoD via Author*)

the conflict was brought down near Starobeshevo, its pilot managing to eject safely. He was recovered by National Guard of Ukraine troops. The separatists made three more claims for Su-25s destroyed that same day, but these were not supported by UkAF reports or photographic or video footage of wreckage.

Four or five of the downed 'Frogfoots' were upgraded Su-25M1s, and two or three more examples sustained combat damage but returned to base.

FIGHTING ISIL MILITANTS IN IRAQ

Su-25 operations in Iraq were rejuvenated in a somewhat surprising manner in late June 2014 thanks to the rapid delivery of a number of ex-RuAF 'Frogfoots', joined shortly thereafter by three Iranian IRG aircraft, in an effort to stop the advance of the forces of the Islamic State of Iraq and Levant (ISIL). The latter had managed to take control of much of northern Syria and then invaded Iraq in June 2014, seizing vast areas in the western part of the country, including the large cities of Mosul and Tikrit. On 30 June ISIL declared it had set up an Islamic state, or caliphate, in the seized territories in Iraq and Syria.

The urgent Su-25 delivery by Russia, agreed in late June, is believed to have comprised ten aircraft. The first five were airlifted to Baghdad International Airport by an RuAF Antonov An-124 on 28 June. Released photographs reveal that all of these were airworthy RuAF aircraft with some service life remaining that had undergone quick pre-delivery structural and system checks at the Kubinka-based 121 Aircraft Repair Plant.

In addition to the ex-Russian 'Frogfoots', three Su-25UBKs and four Su-25Ks were flown from Iran at short notice. Former IrAF machines whose pilots had fled to Iran in 1991, they flew their first combat missions from Imam Ali bin Abi Talib Air Force Base on 1 July. The ex-Iranian Su-25s wore new camouflage and were devoid of national insignia. In addition to being flown in combat, these machines were also used for refresher training for Iraqi pilots with previous Su-25 or Su-22 experience, who would subsequently fly 'Frogfoots' on combat missions against ISIL units. IRG Su-25 pilots were also involved in fighting ISIL, and by the end of July Iranian pilots were reported to have flown more than 40 combat sorties.

Three 'Frogfoots' (one Su-25UBK and two Su-25Ks) previously operated by Iran's IRG are seen here in Iraq devoid of national markings following their arrival in the country on 30 June 2014 as urgent military assistance to fight the advancing forces of ISIL. Almost certainly flown by Iranian aircrews during their first missions in western Iraq, the jets were then handed over to Iraqi pilots following a quick refresher training course (*Iraqi MoD via Author*)

APPENDICES

VVS Su-25 REGIMENTS THAT PROVIDED PERSONNEL FOR SERVICE IN AFGHANISTAN WITH 200th OSAE AND 378th OSHAP

200th OSHAE

1st rotation period
July 1981 to October 1982 at Shindand, with air- and groundcrews from 80th OShAP, home-based at Sital-Chai

2nd rotation period
October 1982 to October 1983 at Shindand, with air- and groundcrews from 80th OShAP, home-based at Sital-Chai

3rd rotation period
October 1983 to October 1984 at Shindand and Bagram, with air- and groundcrews from 80th OShAP, home-based at Sital-Chai

4th rotation period
October 1984 to November 1984 at Bagram, with air- and groundcrews from 90th OShAP, home-based at Tiraspol

378th OSHAP

1st rotation period
1st AE – November 1984 to October 1985 at Bagram, with air- and groundcrews from 90th OShAP, home-based at Tiraspol
2nd AE – November 1984 to October 1985 at Kandahar, with air- and groundcrews from 80th OShAP, home-based at Sital-Chai

2nd rotation period
1st AE – October 1985 to October 1986 at Bagram, with air-and groundcrews from 90th OShAP, home-based at Artsiz
2nd AE – October 1985 to February 1986 at Kandahar and from February 1986 to October 1986 at Bagram, with air- and groundcrews from 90th OShAP, home-based at Artsiz
3rd AE – February 1986 to March 1987 at Kandahar, with air- and groundcrews from 80th OShAP, home-based at Sital-Chai

3rd rotation period
1st AE – October 1986 to October 1987 at Bagram, with air- and groundcrews from 368th OShAP, home-based at Kalinov
2nd AE – October 1986 to October 1987 at Bagram, with air- and groundcrews from 368th OShAP, home-based at Kalinov
3rd AE – March 1987 to February 1988 at Kandahar, with air- and groundcrews from 80th OShAP, home-based at Sital-Chai, and 90th OShAP, home-based at Artsiz

4th rotation period
1st AE – October 1987 to October 1988 at Bagram, with air- and groundcrews from 187th OShAP, home-based at Chernigovka
2nd AE – October 1986 to October 1987 at Bagram, with air- and groundcrews from 187th OShAP, home-based at Chernigovka
3rd AE – March 1988 to February 1989 at Kandahar, with air- and groundcrews from 80th OShAP, home-based at Sital-Chai, 368th OShAP, home-based at Kalinov, and 80th OShAP, home-based at Sital-Chai

5th rotation period
1st AE – October 1988 to February 1989 at Bagram, with air- and groundcrews from 296th OShAP, home-based at Kobrin, and 90th OShAP, home-based at Artsiz
2nd AE – October 1988 to February 1989 at Bagram, with air- and groundcrews from 296th OShAP, home-based at Kobrin, and 90th OShAP, home-based at Artsiz

VVS AND RUAF Su-25 REGIMENTS IN COMBAT IN GEORGIA, TAJIKISTAN, CHECHNYA AND SOUTH OSSETIA

186th IShAP, Buturlinovka
899th Guards ShAP, Buturlinovka (in June 1993 it inherited aircraft and personnel of 186th IShAP)
802nd UAP, Krasnodar
461st ShAP, Krasnodar (in June 1993 it inherited aircraft and personnel of 3rd AE of 802nd UAP)
368th ShAP, Budennovsk
6th ShAP, Taganrog
960th ShAP, Primorsko-Akhtarsk (in 1996 it inherited aircraft and personnel of 13th ShAP)
87th ShAP, Chernigovka
8th GShAP, Galyonki
266th ShAP, Step
4th TsBPiPLS, Lipetsk

COLOUR PLATES

1
T8-1D prototype 'Yellow 81' of the Sukhoi Design Bureau, Shindand, Afghanistan, June 1980

The T8-1D prototype, wearing the bort (serial) number 'Yellow 81', is depicted here in the colours and markings it wore during Operation *Romb* in Afghanistan, which took place between 18 April and 6 June 1980 from Shindand airfield. The first Su-25 prototype, the T8-1 had made its maiden flight on 22 February 1975 in the capable hands of the Sukhoi Design Bureau's famous chief test pilot, Vladimir Ilyushin. After being re-engined with R-95Sh turbojets and undergoing a range of extensive airframe and systems alterations, it was re-designated T8-1D, taking to the air for the first time in its new guise on 21 June 1978.

2
Su-25 c/n 01024/'05' of 200th OShAE, VVS, Shindand, Afghanistan, July 1981

This aircraft, built to the 1st Series production standard, was rolled out of Aircraft Plant No 31 at Tbilisi in early 1981. Initially taken on strength by 80th OShAP at Sital-Chai in April of that year, in July 1981 it was handed over to 200th OShAE and deployed to Shindand, remaining in use in-theatre until November 1984.

3
Su-25 c/n 05027/'37' of 2nd AE/378th OShAP, VVS, Kandahar, Afghanistan, October 1984

This 5th Series production series standard aircraft was rolled out in 1984 and originally delivered to 2nd AE of 387th OShAP, permanently based at Kandahar airfield, in October 1984. It remained in use with this squadron, re-designated 3rd AE in February 1985, until the second half of 1987.

4
Su-25 c/n 06016/'26' of 1st AE/378th OShAP, VVS, Bagram, Afghanistan, April 1986

This 6th Series production standard aircraft was flown by Lt Col Alexander Rutskoy, CO of 378th OShAP. The machine was lost in action on 6 April 1986 during a strike against the Zhawar (Djavara) 'superbase' complex on the border between Afghanistan and Pakistan while performing post-strike reconnaissance with a Filin photo pod, based on the body of a rocket pod and fitted with A-39 wet-film cameras. The pilot managed to eject at the last possible second from the uncontrollable aircraft and was promptly rescued by an Afghanistan National Army infantry unit operating in the area.

5
Su-25 c/n 07063/'47' of 3rd AE/378th OShAP, VVS, Kandahar, Afghanistan, October 1987

This 7th Series production standard aircraft was being flown by Lt Pyotr Golubtsov of 3rd AE/378th OShAP, based at Kandahar, when it was badly damaged by a Stinger hit near the base on 24 October 1987. The machine was performing a CAS mission at the time, the jet being armed with six UB-32M pods for firing S-5 57 mm rockets. Struck during his first attacking pass, Golubtsov managed to retain control of the heavily damaged aircraft and perform a safe landing at Kandahar. After a long repair *in situ* under an experimental programme aimed at assessing aircraft reparability in the event of such heavy damage, the jet was eventually returned to service.

6
Su-25 c/n 08033/'23' of 1st AE/ 378th OShAP, VVS, Bagram, Afghanistan, July 1987

This 8th Series production standard aircraft was being flown by Maj Anatoliy Obedkov of 1st AE/378th OShAP when it took a Stinger hit near Surubi Dam on 28 July 1987 during a low-level convoy-hunting mission. Despite the jet being badly damaged, the pilot succeeded in making an emergency landing at Kabul airfield. Deemed to be beyond repair, the aircraft was written off and subsequently handed over to the Sukhoi Design Bureau for a detailed examination of the combat damage and an assessment of the effectiveness of the self-protection features introduced on 8th Series production standard Su-25s.

7
Su-25 c/n 09083/'Red 09' of 1st AE/378th OShAP, VVS, Bagram, Afghanistan, July 1987

A 9th Series production standard aircraft, c/n 09083 was delivered to 378th OShAP in April 1987. It was among the first Su-25s in the regiment to feature the new-style 'Afghani' camouflage, tailored to blend in with the terrain over which the 'Frogfoots' were flying. The two-tone sand-and-stone colour scheme featured a larger proportion of light blue applied to the fuselage sides than had previously been seen on European-camouflage jets.

8
Su-25UB c/n 38220113117/'Red 63' of 3rd AE/378th OShAP, VVS, Kandahar, Afghanistan, November 1988

This two-seater was among four newly built examples taken on strength by 378th OShAP in October 1988. Two were assigned to 1st AE at Bagram and the other two to 3rd AE at Kandahar. The two-seaters wore a different colour scheme to that of their single-seat counterparts, and had the Ulan-Ude Aircraft Plant badge (a Siberian Bear) applied on both sides of the nose. The four two-seaters operated by 378th OShAP in Afghanistan also had non-standard enhanced armour protection for the rear cockpit in the form of scabbed-on armoured steel side plates.

9
Su-25 c/n 10077/'Red 54' of 1st AE/378th OShAP, VVS, Bagram, Afghanistan, July 1988

A 10th Series production standard aircraft, c/n 10077 sports the full package of self-protection modifications. Delivered to 378th OShAP in September 1987, it has the latest-style Afghan camouflage and displays the traditional 'Grach' (Rook) badge that was initially introduced during the first personnel rotation with 378th OShAP in 1984-85. The jet also has three white stars painted below the canopy, probably denoting successful launches of laser-guided missiles.

10
Su-25UB 'Red 32' of 186th IShAP, RuAF, Gudauta, Abkhazia, March 1993

This was one of a pair of two-seaters operated by 186th IShAP's detachment at Gudauta, in the Georgian breakaway province of Abkhazia, along with six single-seaters – the two-seaters saw use in both combat and training missions. This particular machine was taken on strength by the instructor training regiment, home-based at Buturlinovka, in Russia, in January 1990. During the deployment it wore a large Russian tricolour flag on the fin as a rapid identification measure to distinguish RuAF 'Frogfoots' from the Su-25s operated by the GeAF in combat in Abkhazia.

11
Su-25K 'Red 06' of 3rd AE/802nd UAP, RuAF, Gudauta, Abkhazia, May 1993

This Su-25K was one of 12 undelivered export model 'Frogfoots' used by the RuAF following the break-up of the Soviet Union. These aircraft, delivered in the mid-1980s and operated by 3rd AE of 802nd UAP, were originally used to train foreign pilots at the Krasnodar Higher Pilot School. For operations in Abkhazia between March and November 1993, the deployed Su-25Ks and Su-25UBs at Gudauta were given rapid visual identification markings in the form of a large tricolour Russian flag applied on both sides of the fin. This jet also had its wingtip pods painted blue, white and green.

12
Su-25BM 'Red 32' of 186th IShAP, RuAF, Kokayty, Uzbekistan, April 1993

This 'sharkmouthed' RuAF Su-25BM belonged to 186th IShAP, which was transformed into 899th GShAP in June 1993. The aircraft saw combat use during the civil war in Tajikistan in 1992-93, operating from Kokayty in Uzbekistan. This particular aircraft was lost in May 2005 during a deployment to Dushanbe-Aini, in Tajikistan. Maj Vladimir Pryadchenko of 899th ShAP reported an in-flight emergency when the jet caught fire during a training mission. He ejected successfully, and the aircraft hit the ground 15.5 miles from Dushanbe-Aini.

13
Su-25 'White 51' of 187th ShAP, RuAF, Kant, Kyrgyzstan, July 2004

An RuAF Su-25 of 187th ShAP, home-based at Chernigovka in Russia's Far East, this aircraft operated over Tajikistan from Kant airfield, in Kyrgyzstan, where the 203rd Russian Military Base was established in October 2003. It displays a distinctive 'sharksmouth', the Russian tricolour flag at the top of both sides of the rudder and Afghanistan-era Grach (Rook) badges on both engine nacelles.

14
Su-25BM 'Red 59' of 368th ShAP, RuAF, Budennovsk, Russia, July 2000

An RuAF Su-25BM of 368th ShAP, home-based at Budennovsk in Russia's southern region, this was a 10th Series production standard machine from a batch of 50 built in 1990. Originally intended for target-towing, they had uprated R-195 turbojets and improved navigation equipment. In late 1990 368th ShAP inherited 11 Su-25BMs originally delivered in May-August of that year to 65th OBAE (*Otdel'naya Bombardirovochnaya Aviatsionnaya Eskadrilya* – Independent Dive-Bomber Aviation Squadron), an independent target-towing squadron stationed at Damgarten, in Germany, and disbanded in November 1990. This aircraft saw combat in the second Chechen war with 368th ShAP.

15
Su-25UB 'Red 21' of 1st AE/461st ShAP, RuAF, Mozdok, Russia, September 1999

This two-seat 'Frogfoot' took part in the second campaign in Chechnya between 1999 and 2001. On both sides of its nose it wore the famous 'Chained Dog' badge created by a pilot of 461st ShAP, home-based at Krasnodar, and subsequently applied to both single- and two-seat Su-25s assigned to the regiment's two component squadrons, the first aircraft receiving it in 1998.

16
Su-25SM 'Red 05' of 368th ShAP, RuAF, Budennovsk, Russia, August 2008

This upgraded 'Frogfoot' of 368th ShAP, stationed at Budennovsk, was among the few examples to participate in the short conflict in South Ossetia in August 2008. The regiment had only received its first batch of six Su-25SMs the previous year, and one of these aircraft was shot down during the fighting in South Ossetia. Two more upgraded machines were badly damaged when hit by Igla shoulder-launched SAMs, but their pilots managed to return to base.

17
Su-25K 'Red 46' of 461st ShAP, RuAF, Budennovsk, Russia, August 2008

An export-standard machine, this aircraft was used in the war with Georgia over the disputed territory of South Ossetia in August 2008. Forward-deployed to Budennovsk, the jet was badly damaged by a SAM hit in the port engine on 11 August. Its pilot, Maj Ivan Konukhov, managed to land the aeroplane at Mozdok. Subsequently, the jet was handed over to the 121st Aviation Repair Plant at Kubinka near Moscow, where it underwent a detailed damage assessment after being deemed beyond economical repair.

18
Su-25UB 'Red 92' of 187th ShAP, RuAF, Kant, Kyrgyzstan, July 2005

This two-seater of 187th ShAP, home-based at Chernigovka, in Russia's Far East, participated in a deployment to the 302nd Russian Military Base at Kant in Kyrgyzstan in 2005. It boasted impressive artwork, including a 'sharksmouth', the Ulan-Ude Aircraft Plant's trademark Siberian Bear logo on both sides of the nose, the traditional Grach (Rook) badge dating from the Afghanistan-war era and the Russian tricolour flag at the top of the rudder on both sides.

19
Su-25 'Red 27' of 960th ShAP, RuAF, Primorsko-Akhtarsk, Russia, May 2009

Assigned to 960th ShAP, home-based at Primorsko-Akhtarsk in southern Russia, this 'Frogfoot' sported perhaps the most colourful scheme to be found on an RuAF aircraft. Several non-standard colours were applied to the airframe over a period of time, including the blue wingtip pods, under-nose fuel tank and wing pylon tips. The leading edges of the wings, tailplane and fin were also painted blue. A distinctive 'sharksmouth' adorned both sides of the nose, the Sukhoi logo was displayed on the fin and a 960th ShAP badge (a lion's head) was carefully applied to the engine intakes. Its bort number was repeated at the top of the fin and on the front of each wing pylon.

20
Su-25T 'Red 84' of 2nd AE/760th ISIAP, RuAF, Lipetsk, Russia, May 2008

Assigned to 760th ISIAP, home-based at Lipetsk, in Russia, this aircraft was one of two used in anger during the second war in Chechnya in September-December 1999. The two 'Super Frogfoots' were forward-deployed to Mozdok airfield and mainly fired Kh-25ML and Kh-29L laser-guided missiles against a number of high-value pre-planned targets in the troubled republic.

21
Su-25KM 'Blue 18' of the Attack Squadron, Georgian Air Force, Marneuli, Georgia, August 2008

This aircraft was assigned to the sole Georgian attack squadron, home-based at Marneuli. In the mid-2000s it was upgraded to KM standard, also known as the Scorpion, a joint project by the Georgian aircraft manufacturer TAM and Elbit Systems of Israel to digitalise and Westernise the 'Frogfoot'. Four upgraded Su-25KMs were on strength with the GeAF by the outbreak of the August 2008 war in South Ossetia, but only one was actually used in combat, performing a solitary attack on a Russian Army column on the road between Djava and Tskhinvali on the morning of 8 August.

22
Su-25K 'Black 56' of the Iran Islamic Revolutionary Guards, Tehran, Iran, August 2010
Assigned to the fleet of the Iran Islamic Revolutionary Guards' aviation force, this Su-25K was originally delivered to the Iraqi Air Force and took part in the closing stages of the war with Iran. During the Gulf War in January 1991 its pilot flew it to Iran, where the jet was restored to airworthy condition in the late 2000s and issued with the IRG at Tehran-Mehrabad airport.

23
Su-25K c/n 25590 of the Iraqi Air Force, Baghdad, Iraq, May 1989
Iraq was an early export customer for the 'Frogfoot', with total deliveries amounting to 69 Su-25K single-seaters and four Su-25UBK two-seaters according to Russian sources. These machines were camouflaged with two shades of brown and light blue undersurfaces. They also displayed large Iraqi flags on either side of their fins. By the end of the 1980s, when the second batch of Su-25s had been delivered, the 'Frogfoots' equipped at least three operational squadrons, the 109th, 115th and 119th. Two IrAF Su-25Ks were reportedly lost while conducting combat missions during the conflict with Iran.

24
Su-25K 'Red B-18' of the 2nd Squadron/26th Fighter-Bomber Regiment, Força Aérea Nacional Angolana, Namib, Angola, 1990
This Angolan Su-25K was one of 12 single-seaters and a pair of two-seaters taken on strength in early 1988 by the 2nd Squadron of the 26th Fighter-Bomber Regiment, stationed at Namib airfield. The aircraft is camouflaged in two shades of brown, with light blue applied to its undersurfaces and fuselage sides.

25
Su-25UB c/n 38220113522/'Grey 120' of the 101st Squadron/Air Wing, Macedonian Air Force, Petrovec, Macedonia, June 2001
An early production aircraft, this two-seater was previously operated by the Belarusian Air Force. It was one of four two-seat 'Frogfoots' originally delivered to 378th OShAP at Bagram, wearing the original number '60', in October 1988 – this was replaced shortly after its delivery by '64' to avoid number duplication with a single-seater. It had scabbed-on steel armour plates fitted to either side of the rear cockpit for additional pilot protection.

26
Su-25 'Red 02' of the Force Aerienne de Cote d'Ivoire, Abidjan, Ivory Coast, October 2004
Displaying a large 'sharksmouth', this aircraft was one of a pair of single-seat Su-25s previously operated by the Belarusian Air Force and sold to the Ivory Coast, together with two Su-25UB two-seaters, in 2004. The entire 'Frogfoot' fleet was effectively neutralised on the ramps and in the hangars at Yamoussoukro and Abidjan airfields by French Special Forces following the notorious S-5 rocket attack on a French military camp by both two-seaters on 6 November 2004.

27
Su-25 'White FG-500' of the 2nd Tactical Air Group, Air Force of the Democratic Republic of the Congo, Kamina, Democratic Republic of Congo, June 2001
This aircraft was one of four factory-fresh Su-25s purchased from TAM by the Democratic Republic of Congo (formerly Zaire) in 1999-2000 and used in the internal conflict in the country.

28
Su-25UB '087' of the Esquadron 112/Grupo Aeroe 11, Fuerza Aérea del Perú, Talara, July 2001
This Su-25UB two-seater was one of two Peruvian 'Frogfoots' upgraded to use the Kh-58U anti-radiation missile, seen here under its wing. This missile is used in conjunction with the KRK-UO underfuselage targeting pod and the L150 radar-warning receiver, enabling the Su-25 to be employed in the demanding Suppression of Enemy Air Defence role. Of the 18 'Frogfoots' supplied to Peru in 1998 only four are presently believed to be serviceable.

29
Su-25 'Black 203' of the Sudanese Air Force, El Fashir, Sudan, August 2010
This aircraft was amongst a batch of 14 second-hand 'Frogfoots' purchased by Sudan from Belarus in 2009-10. Based at El Fashir airport, they have reportedly been used to attack rebel targets in the Darfur, where civil war has been raging since 2003.

30
Su-25UBK 'Red 70' of the 121st Ground-Attack Aviation Squadron, Armenian Air Force, Gumri, Armenia, August 2005
An export-standard two-seater, this was one of the two Su-25UBKs donated by Russia and supplied clandestinely in late 1992, along with six Su-25K single-seaters taken from the inventory of 802nd UAP, home-based at Krasnodar.

31
Su-25K 'Black 56' of the Iraqi Air Force, Imam Ali bin Abi Talib Air Force Base, Iraq, July 2014
This single-seater was originally delivered to the IrAF in the late 1980s, and it was one of seven examples that managed to flee Iraq into neighbouring Iran in February 1991 during Operation Desert Storm. Five of these single-seaters were returned to airworthy condition after spending between 13 to 15 years in storage and handed over to the IRG's air service, this particular jet being given the serial number 15-2456 (see profile 22). It was one of two single-seaters returned to the IrAF on 30 June 2014 in the wake of the ISIL invasion of Iraq.

32
Su-25UBK 'Black 58' of the Iraqi Air Force, Imam Ali bin Abi Talib Air Force Base, Iraq, July 2014
This two-seater is also a former Iranian IRG aircraft, originally serialled 15-2458. It too was delivered to Iraq on 30 June 2014 as urgent military aid from Iran to be used against the advancing forces of ISIL. The two-seater, featuring an upgraded nav/attack suite of Iranian origin, was reportedly followed into IrAF service by two more IRG Su-25UBKs.

33
Su-25 'Blue 25' of the 299th Tactical Aviation Brigade, Nikolayev-Kulbakino, Ukraine, summer 2014
At the outbreak of the civil war in Ukraine in April 2014, the UkAF had a fleet of some 70 'Frogfoots', including ten upgraded examples. Only about 15 of these jets were airworthy, however, and six of these were lost in combat in June and July 2014. 'Blue 25', a non-upgraded aircraft that had been grounded in September 2013, was urgently returned to airworthy condition following the heavy losses suffered by the UkAF. It has since seen combat in Ukraine's easternmost provinces with the 299th TAB.

INDEX

Page references in **bold** refer to illustrations; and e.g. 'cp. **11** (38, 94)' refers to a colour profile, with the profile page and the plate commentary page in brackets.

Abkhazia cp.**10–11** (38, 93–94), 59, 62–67
Afghanistan 10–58, **16**, cp.**1–9** (35–37, 93), 92
aircraft
  Mi-24 **21**
  MiG21bis **18**
  Su-22 **84**
  Su-25 **9**, **21**
  Su-25 '02' **33**
  Su-25 '03' **18**
  Su-25 '06' **46**, **50**, **51**
  Su-25 '22' **29**
  Su-25 '34' **24**
  Su-25 'Black 203' cp.**29** (44, 95)
  Su-25 'Blue 25' cp.**33** (45, 95)
  Su-25 c/n 01024/'05' cp.**2** (35, 93)
  Su-25 c/n 05027/'37' cp.**3** (35, 93)
  Su-25 c/n 06016/'26' **23**, cp.**4** (36, 93)
  Su-25 c/n 07063/'47' **34**, cp.**5** (36, 93)
  Su-25 c/n 08033/'23' **32**, cp.**6** (36, 93)
  Su-25 c/n 09083/'Red 09' cp.**7** (37, 93)
  Su-25 c/n 10077/'Red 54' cp.**9** (37, 93)
  Su-25 'Red 02' cp.**26** (43, 95)
  Su-25 'Red 27' cp.**19** (41, 94)
  Su-25 'White 51' cp.**13** (39, 94)
  Su-25 'White FG-500' cp.**27** (43)
  Su-25BM **64**, **78**
  Su-25BM '55' **77**
  Su-25BM 'Red 32' cp.**12** (38, 94)
  Su-25BM 'Red 59' cp.**14** (39, 94)
  Su-25K '28' **63**
  Su-25K '34' **63**
  Su-25K '46' **79**, **81**, **91**
  Su-25K 25616 (c/n 10310) **82**
  Su-25K 'Black 56' cp.**22** (42, 95), cp.**31** (45, 95)
  Su-25K c/n 25590 cp.**23** (42, 95)
  Su-25K 'Red 06' cp.**11** (38, 94)
  Su-25K 'Red 46' cp.**17** (40, 94)
  Su-25K 'Red B-18' cp.**24** (42, 95)
  Su-25KM 'Blue 18' cp.**21** (41, 94–95)
  Su-25SM **74**
  Su-25SM '08' **79**
  Su-25SM '09' **80**, **80**
  Su-25SM 'Red 05' cp.**16** (40, 94)
  Su-25M1 **87**, **87**
  Su-25T **9**, **76**
  Su-25T 'Red 84' cp.**20** (41, 94)
  Su-25UB **8**, **62**
  Su-25UB '087' cp.**28** (44, 95)
  Su-25UB c/n 38220113117/'Red 63' cp.**8** (37, 93)
  Su-25UB c/n 38220113522/'Grey 120' cp.**25** (43, 95)
  Su-25UB 'Red 21' cp.**15** (39, 94)
  Su-25UB 'Red 32' cp.**10** (38, 93)
  Su-25UB 'Red 92' cp.**18** (40, 94)
  Su-25UBK **60**, **91**
  Su-25UBK 'Black 58' cp.**32** (45, 95)
  Su-25UBK 'Red 70' cp.**30** (44, 95)
  T8-1 **6**, **7**
  T8-1D 10–11, **11**
  T8-1D prototype 'Yellow 81' cp.**1** (35, 93)
  T8-3 7–8, 10–11
  T8-4 **7**
Alexandrov, Capt Mikhail 49
Alfyorov, Maj Gen Vladimir 11, 12, 13
Alyoshin, 1Lt Igor 31, **31**
Angola cp.**24** (42, 95), 82, **82**

Araslanov, Maj Alexander 51–53, 53–54, 54–55, 56
Armenia cp.**30** (44, 95), 59, 60–62
armour 8, 9, cp.**8** (37, 93)
Azerbaijan 59, 60–62

badges and insignia **21**, cp.**9** (37, 93), cp.**15** (39, 94), cp.**18** (40, 94), cp.**19** (41, 94)
Bagram airfield **22**, **23**, 52
bombs and bombing
  in Abkhazia 66
  in Afghanistan 11, 12, 13, 14, 17–18, **22**, 54–55, **54**
  in Chechnya 75, 76
  FAB-250 **7**
  FAB-500M54 **23**
  FAB-500M62 75
  illumination 26
  ODAB-500P thermobaric 19, 75
  OFAB-250M-54 **87**, **88**
Bondaryov, Maj Gen Viktor **70**
Borisuk, Col Sergey 73–74
Burak, Capt Miroslav 31, **31**

Chechnya 4, cp.**14** (39, 94), cp.**20** (41, 94), 59, 70–76, 92
cockpits **9**
combat survivability features 8–9, 11
Congo, Democratic Republic of cp.**27** (43, 95), 84, **84**

Edamenkov, Maj Vladimir 78–79
ejecting 43–48, **58**
Emelyushin, Capt Sergey 50, 51
engines 9, 14, **50**
Ethiopian-Eritrean War (1998-2000) 82–83

fuel tanks **7**, 18, **84**

Georgia cp.**21** (41, 94–95), 59, 61, 62–67, 76–80, 92
Golovanov, Col Alexander 62
Golubtsov, 1Lt Pyotr 34, **34**, 93
Goncharenko, 1Lt Vladislav **26**, **27**
Gritskevich, 1Lt Sergey **26**, 28
Grozny Presidential Palace 71, **71**
guns, VPU-17A 7, **8**, 18, **49**

Ilyushin, Vladimir 7, 93
Ingushetia 59, 60
Iran cp.**22** (42, 95), 85, **86**
Iran-Iraq War (1980-88) cp.**22** (42, 95), 81
Iraq cp.**23** (42, 95), cp.**31** (45, 95), cp.**32** (45, 95), **81**, 82, **82**, **90**, 91, **91**
Ivanov, Alexander 10, 12
Ivory Coast cp.**26** (43, 95), 84–85, **85**

Kabul airport **56**
Kandahar airfield **28**, **57**
Kant air base **69**
Kobilash, Col Sergey 77, **77**, 78
Kononenko, 1Lt T 24
Konukhov, Maj Ivan 79, 94
Koshkin, 1Lt Alexander 30, 46, 47–48, 49–50, 60, 61, 65–66, 71–72
Kudryavtsev, 1Lt Andrey 51, 53
Kurbanov, Lt Vaghit 60–61

Macedonia cp.**25** (43, 95), 83, **83**
Mazar-e-Sharif airfield **24**
military airlifters **90**
mine-laying 18, 24, 30, 68
missiles 11, 25–26, 76
  Kh-25ML 25, **76**
  Kh-29L 25, **25**, **76**

Kh-58U cp.**28** (44, 95), **83**
protection against 28–29
R-60 **63**, 68, **86**
SAMs 28, 30, 33
Muzika, Valeriy 10, 12, 13, **13**, **14**

Nagorni Karabakh 60–61
navigation/attack systems 74, 75–76, 83
Nechaev, Capt Ivan 79–80
night combat sorties 26–27

Obedkov, Maj Anatoliy 32–33, 48, 93
Ossetia cp.**16** (40, 94), cp.**17** (40, 94), cp.**21** (41, 94–95), 59, 60, 76–80, 92

Pakistan raid (1986) 49–50
Paltusov, 1Lt Vladimir 31, **31**
Pavlov, Capt Mikhail 4, 63–64, **63**, 65, 68, 75
Pavlykov, 1Lt Konstantin 29, **30**, 31–32, **31**
Peru cp.**28** (44, 95), 83, **83**, **84**
Pryadchenko, Maj Vladimir 69, 94

rockets 11, 17, 75, 76
  B8M **7**, **33**, **63**
  B8M1 **69**, **86**, **88**
  S-8 **86**, 89
  S-24 **17**, **59**, **63**
  S-25 **64**
  S-250FM **87**
  UB-32M **23**
RuAF units
  4th TsPLSiBP 76, **76**, 92
  16th ShAP 70–76, 92
  18th GShAP 68, 69, 92
  80th OShAP 62
  186th IShAP cp.**10** (38, 93), cp.**12** (38, 94), 64, 65, 67–68, 92
  187th ShAP cp.**13** (39, 94), cp.**18** (40, 94), 69, 92
  266th ShAP 69, 92
  368th ShAP cp.**14** (39, 94), cp.**16** (40, 94), 70–80, 92
  461st ShAP cp.**15** (39, 94), 68, 70–76, 79–80, 92
  760th ISIAP cp.**20** (41, 94)
  802nd UAP cp.**11** (38, 94), 60, 61, 63–64, 64–67, 92
  899th ShAP 68, **68**, 69, 92, 94
  960th ShAP cp.**19** (41, 94), **59**, 73, 76, 92
Ruban, Maj Pyotr 20–21, **20**
Rutskoy, Col Alexander 25, 27, 53, **53**, 93
Ryabov, Maj Eduard 48
Rybakov, Maj Alexander 33–34, **33**, 46–47, 49

Savtchenko, Ivan 6
Shulimov, Maj 46, 47–48
Solovyov, Vladimir 10, **14**
Strepetov, Lt Col Grigoriy 33–34, 46, 48–49, **48**
Sudan cp.**29** (44, 95), 85–86, **86**

Tajikistan cp.**12** (38, 94), cp.**13** (39, 94), 59, 67–69, 92
Terebunskiy, Lt Col Oleg 77–78
Tskhinvali **78**

Ukraine cp.**33** (45, 95), 87–91, **87**, **88**

VVS units
  80th OShAP 15, 93
  200th OShAE 15–21, cp.**2** (35, 93), 92
  378th OShAP 21–58, cp.**3–9** (35–37, 93), 92

Yakovlev, Capt Alexander **63**

Zemlyakov, 1 Lt Viktor 31, **31**